THE STAGE IN ULSTER FROM THE EIGHTEENTH CENTURY

selected from the theatre archive
of the Linen Hall Library

OPHELIA BYRNE

1997
The Linen Hall Library
Belfast

Published 1997 by
The Linen Hall Library
17 Donegall Square North
Belfast BT1 5GD.

© *Ophelia Byrne, 1997*

ISBN 1 900921 057

Printed by W. & G. Baird Ltd. at the Greystone Press, Antrim.

The Linen Hall Library acknowledges the financial assistance of the Cultural
Traditions Programme of the Northern Ireland Community Relations Council,
which aims to encourage acceptance and understanding of cultural diversity.

Contents

Introduction

The Theatre Archive of the Linen Hall Library consists of a collection of several thousand items, the earliest of which date back to the eighteenth century. These have been donated over the years by members of the theatrical and wider communities. Though termed the 'Theatre Archive' by tradition, the scope of the UTC has grown to include all of the performing arts, including dance, opera, and music of all sorts. The bedrock of the archive to date, however, remains its theatre collection. All forms of material which help to record the performing arts experience are included in the holding, such as programmes, posters, scrapbooks, press cuttings, letters, manuscript plays, typescript plays, audiovisual items, handbills, photographs and designs.

This book is a work-in-progress guide to those companies and theatres for whom material is held in the Theatre Archive. As such, the scale of each entry generally relates to the amount of material available in the collection. Included in chronological order are overviews of the stage in Ulster in the eighteenth and nineteenth centuries. Given the diversification of the theatre experience in the twentieth century, it was felt more useful for this period to provide individual accounts of the origins of various theatres and theatre companies. The final item in the guide is a catalogue for the archive's introductory exhibition, *The Stage in Ulster*.

It is hoped that this will be a useful research source, offering brief, factual information to those with a general interest in theatre. Researchers wishing to consult the archive material are referred to the detailed archive catalogue also prepared this year. This gives details of the library holding for companies and theatres, and will be regularly updated. It also includes full production lists, compiled for archive purposes, for the following groups to date: the Northern Drama League, the Little Theatre, the Playhouse, the Ulster Group Theatre (1940–1960), the Arts Theatre (1950–1971), the Lyric Players Theatre, Field Day Theatre Company and Charabanc Theatre Company.

The Library owes particular thanks to the Cultural Traditions Programme of the Northern Ireland Community Relatioins Council, whose funding of the John Boyd Fellowship in Theatre Archive 1996/7 has made the work to date possible. This has also revealed the need for, and the potential of, systematic commitment to the field, and the library is currently planning long-term provision for what will become its Theatre and Performing Arts Archive. In this respect support already received from Belfast City Council and the Lloyds TSB Foundation for Northern Ireland has been of signal assistance.

The existing strength of the Collection owes much to past donations, and with the archive now destined to receive its place in the lime-light, its future will also depend on contact with, and the generosity of, those involved in theatre and the performing arts. If, indeed, your group is not included here, do contact us, and we can ensure that the record is set straight for posterity.

On a personal note, I would like to thank John Boyd, and my supervisors for the year, John Killen and David Grant. I would also like to acknowledge my debt to Sam Hanna Bell's 1972 publication, *The Theatre in Ulster*.

THE EIGHTEENTH CENTURY

Mr KEAN

as Richard the III.d

Pub.d by J Lodge Dawson S.t

... the Stage,
Becomes the pride of this enlighten'd Age...[1]

The theatre swept into eighteenth century Ulster with such vigour that its popularity in both the performance and literary spheres was established for some six decades. The first recorded performances took place at Newry and Belfast in 1736, when the Smock Alley troupe from Dublin travelled to the north of Ireland for a summer season. Thereafter, both published and performed drama became extremely popular, and until the end of the century Ulster supported both aspects with ease. Some fifty locally printed playscripts in the archive testify to the fact that dramatic literature was regularly produced and sold in Ulster; J.R.R. Adams indicates that the main market for this was Belfast and the larger towns 'which could afford a theatre'.[2] This suggests that a lively and literate local audience existed for the theatre; regular reprints of plays such as Thomas Sheridan's *The Brave Irishman, or Captain O'Blunder*, and *The Mock Doctor, or the Dumb Lady Cur'd* testify to the enduring popularity of the script. However, many of these are not of a local nature. If it is true that 'Dublin was almost totally dependent on London for its theatrical material'[3], play lists show that the theatre in Ulster was no less so. Though some of the scripts certainly came via Dublin, the title pages of plays printed in Belfast very often refer to performances at the London theatres. This accords with Clark's view that, while Cork, Limerick, Waterford and Newry became satellites of Dublin at this time, Belfast did not. It ultimately emerged as an independent theatre centre and attached Londonderry as a satellite.[4] In this capacity, a sparkling season at Dublin or Londonderry would include the London successes, and depending on the acumen of the theatre manager, the script of the latest London success could travel remarkably quickly to Ireland. Goldsmith's *She Stoops to Conquer*, for example, was presented in Belfast just six months after its London première in 1773, and was printed in the town not long afterwards. Such rapidity was not unique, and was greatly facilitated by the complex laws then extant on both printed and performance copyright in relation to dramatic compositions.

The Playwright and Copyright

One notable absence on the title pages of the eighteenth century scripts is a notification of copyright. Eighteenth century law in relation to performance rights provided little protection for the playwright. In neither Ireland nor England did an author's proprietary right in a dramatic performance exist until 1833 and so, plays could be performed until that date without payment of fees to the writer. Benefits were, instead, awarded to authors on the third, sixth, ninth etc. performances, but only during the first run of a new play.[5] However, publishing rights, in England at least, were quite different, as is illustrated by a famous case, *Macklin v. Richardson*. Macklin, a successful playwright, was determined to protect the rights to his farce *Love a la Mode*. Hence, though allowing the play to be performed, Macklin did not print or publish the work. Even when it was performed, Macklin arranged to have prompt copies of the play removed at the end of each show, and he required actors to pay for use of the play at their own benefit performances. Consequently, the play acquired curiosity value, and the defendants, who were proprietors of a magazine, employed a short-hand writer to take down the words of the play at the theatre. They thereafter published the first act, and promised subsequently to publish the second. In so doing, Macklin had lost his publishing rights. In addition, as the play could now be performed without his permission, he would no longer earn performance rights either. The playwright therefore sought an injunction against the magazine. This was granted by Lord Commissioner Smythe. In making his judgement, the Commissioner 'negatived the idea that acting a play is a publication of it.'[6] In theory, then, the playwright now retained exclusive rights to the publication of his play. In addition, until the play was published, he had some control over performances, as no others had the right to issue scripts in printed form. In practice, however, such rights were only applicable if all parties behaved according to the letter of the law. If *Macklin v. Richardson* testifies to the sheer popularity of the written drama, it also makes clear the difficulties endured by writers, and the extreme methods which could be used to enable publication of the more popular scripts.

The playwright in Ireland

Though all of these factors were certainly applicable to Ireland, the *Macklin v. Richardson* case ruling was not. The legal protection afforded to literary property by the British Copyright Act of 1709 did not extend to Ireland, and only after the Act of Union was Ireland, under the Copyright Act of 1801, forced to recognise the existence of literary property in law.[7] Hence, playwrights received no recompense for the Irish publication of their scripts and, in effect, no rights were paid on either performed or printed versions of a playwright's work in Ireland in the eighteenth century.

While this mitigated severely against the playwright, it also meant that audiences were often provided with very contemporary versions of the productions at the theatres in the metropolis: the archive copy of Edward Young's *The Revenge* is, for example, 'Marked with the variations in the manager's book, at the Theatre-Royal in Drury-Lane'. In addition, there were no negotiation delays or control and copyright wrangles to delay productions of the latest and most fashionable plays. This ensured that the most recent London successes could reach Ulster rapidly.

Local Presentations

Though the provincial playhouses generally conformed to the 'hits' of the metropolis, they also produced 'a not inconsiderable body of original dramatic entertainment'.[8] Some light-hearted local works were presented; for example, *Just Arrived in L'Derry; or, The Thespian from Ennishoen* was performed at Londonderry in 1798. Similar Belfast examples include *The Humours of Belfast*, a two act ballad farce, in 1766; *Harlequin in Derry*, and *The Giant's Causeway; or, A Trip to the Dargle*, in 1770, (each having been adapted for local audiences from pieces performed elsewhere in Ireland); and *Poor Dartry's Trip to Belfast*, a musical recitative, in 1794. Rather more substantial examples were Dr. Maryat's comic opera *Love in a Bog*, presented in Belfast in 1772, and Dr. Bambridge's *The Guillotine; or, the Death of Louis XVI*, staged in 1793 in Belfast.[9] In general, however,

'managers outside the capital did not pursue an avowed policy for the encouragement of local playwrighting... at best, when patriotic passions were at their peak from 1778 to 1798, [they] expressed a romantically neutral Hibernianism on occasion... [and] only sporadically tried to appeal to their audiences with works of Irish content.'[10]

The Performers

William Smith Clark notes in *The Irish Stage in the County Towns* that between 1770 and 1800, Belfast supported 20 winter seasons at the theatre of three to nine months each. From 1773 onwards, these seasons were provided by a resident company. Most performers were based in England and travelled to Ireland to perform on a freelance basis, often touring with a company from place to place during the season. Given the transport circumstances at the time, this was often difficult and time-consuming; John Bernard, an eighteenth century actor, describes a journey undertaken by a Belfast touring company from Londonderry to Sligo:

'...which we reached in every description of vehicle, with the aid of every description of the animal called horse; in every description of weather and upon every description of road – thoroughfares which, to use a permissible pun, we found to be thorough foul... we were bog'd very often, and trusted for instruction to finger-posts which, from the capacity of their clay sockets, blew round like weathercocks, and only pointed right if the wind was...'[11]

Such conditions were not unusual; Bernard calls them 'common characteristics of Irish travelling in those days'.[12] Nevertheless, even actors of the fame of Mrs. Siddons carried on undeterred; she performed in Belfast on June 6, 1785 with the élite of Ulster in the audience. In general, however, audiences were entertained by seasonal resident companies. Managers at this time drew troupes together on different arrangements. Terms for actors depended on their standing in the company. Subscribers, 'managers or principal performers of long standing, normally received a fixed percentage of the nightly profits at the theatre'.[13] Others were paid at a fixed nightly or weekly rate. Benefit performances supplemented this arrangement, whereby each performer in turn took the profit of a night less house costs. For these the actor was expected to make

> 'calls on well-to-do patrons and to solicit the attendance of themselves and their friends. Recipients who, because of disability or ill-health, were unable to make personal visits to patrons often felt obliged to apologise in the newspapers.'[14]

The performer was thus obliged to be the most public of figures, and to interact with his audience at a personal level. The more gregarious company members became part of the life of the town during their stay. John Bernard's *Retrospections* gives an excellent account of the life of a travelling player at this time, noting that at Derry he experienced 'the same cordial and generous reception in private life which had marked my stay at Belfast'. This included meetings with the Bishop of Derry, who was a theatre subscriber, and evenings spent by invitation at Shane's Castle, the home of John O'Neill, and at the Philharmonic Society, Belfast.[15] As a result, Bernard's benefit nights were successful; those of others were not always so, and as the benefit was 'the ultimate harvest',[16] a poor house could signal financial disaster for the performer for that season.

The Theatres

Benefit nights tended to take place late in the season, with the theatre management reserving the earlier, most profitable dates for itself.[17] At its busiest, the Belfast theatre saw thrice-weekly productions (generally Mondays, Wednesdays and Fridays) staged on a repertory system. An evening at the theatre could consist, not only of a main show, or mainpiece, but also of an afterpiece or two, together with entr'acte entertainments of singing, dancing or music. The mainpiece might also be accompanied by a prologue and epilogue, or even ignored in favour of programs composed entirely of short pieces.[18] Hence, for example, the bill on April 10, 1778 at Rosemary Lane consisted of *The tragedy of Jane Shore*, the comedy of *The Man of Quality*, and two farces, *The Honest Yorkshireman* and *Taste*. The evening's entertainment therefore began quite early; Greene and Clark estimate a typical evening at the Dublin theatres could take five to six hours, and most Belfast bills specify opening times of six or seven o'clock.

It is hardly surprising then that the topic of comfort at the theatre was of lively interest to theatre-goers at the time. A notice in the *Belfast News-Letter* of November 2, 1790, for example, described Belfast's Rosemary Lane Theatre as having

> 'quantities of dirt and dust which are suffered to remain for months... the gallery is so ill-ceilinged that quantities of punch and other liquors fall in copious showers on the unoffending heads in the boxes. The

seats consist of ill-planed boards, destitute of covering. In short, everything in the boxes is finished in the shabbiest style.'

Other theatres in Ulster were less neglected. Three main towns, Newry, Belfast and Londonderry, boasted a playhouse in the eighteenth century, and considerable interplay of companies took place between the three. Newry's first playhouse was opened in 1769 at High Street by manager James Parker, but possessed no boxes and limited back stage accommodation.[19] However, Belfast and Dublin touring companies came to play there, and by 1783 Newry was deemed ready for its first purpose-built theatre, the Theatre Royal. This stood at numbers 71–3 Hill Street, and had boxes behind the pit, as well as lower and upper side-boxes.[20] An elegant and luxurious building, it was contrasted most favourably with the Belfast theatre at this time[21] and served the town until 1832. Londonderry, meanwhile, already had its own theatre. Though initially the Great Hall of the Town Hall and Exchange was used for its theatricals, in August 1774 manager Michael Atkins opened a new theatre at the New Row, Ship Quay. This was, however, 'a small, insubstantial building',[22] and so in 1786 Atkins anounced he was building 'an elegant and commodious new theatre which (when finished) will for its magnitude be equal in elegance to any house in the Kingdom.'[23] The new theatre was at Artillery Lane (now Artillery Street), on a 'conspicuous and accessible site'[24] and contained side-boxes.[25] It saw more or less continuous use from its opening in 1789 to the end of the century, with the industrious Atkins, who also then ran the theatre in Belfast, alternating his companies between the two venues according to the civil circumstances of the times. Lisburn, it should be noted, also had a season in 1784, when Atkins transferred his company to the Market House and fixed up its second-floor ballroom as a theatre from August to November.[26]

Belfast supported five consecutive playhouses in the eighteenth century for which there are records: the 'Vaults' (n.d. –1766), the Mill Gate Theatre (1768–1778), the theatre at Rosemary Lane (1784–1792) and the Arthur Street theatre, also called the first Theatre Royal (1793–1871). Again, a steady progression in building standards is evident over the century. The first Belfast theatre is presumed to have been a converted wine vault located in Weigh-house Lane, now absorbed by Victoria Street and an unprepossessing area at the time. The chief Belfast venue for players for 16 years, it was abandoned as inadequate for its purpose in 1766.[27] Its successor, the 'New Theatre in Mill Street', or 'The Theatre, Mill Gate', opened by manager James Parker on August 23, 1768 in an area 'scarcely as respectable as the former'.[28] This building was possibly refurbished in 1770, when an announcement was made of the 'New Theatre in Mill Gate' under the management of one Mr. Ryder. Again, however, this proved only adequate for its purpose, and, like the Vaults, it contained no boxes. Hence, on October 23, 1778, the 'New Theatre in Ann Street' opened, and as it 'possessed boxes, as well as pit and gallery, the new house evidently had more resemblance to an actual theatre than any which preceded it.'[29] John Bernard however, recalls a 'small, infirm and inconvenient'[30] building, and a newspaper notice declared the building 'at times too small for the reception of the audience'.[31] Hence, the theatre manager Michael Atkins, took 'a lot of ground in Rosemary Lane, an excellent and central situation',[32] on which was built a new theatre, adding boxes to the customary pit and gallery. This opened on March 3, 1784 and was initially feted; Atkins delivered an address at its opening, testifying to the increased confidence of the citizens of Belfast in its prosperity:

> Rais'd by the bounty of our Patrons here,
> In a new Theatre we now appear;
> A structure wish'd for this polished Town
> To worth and opulence by virtue grown.
> Divested of licentiousness, the Stage,
> Becomes the pride of this enlighten'd Age...
> this structure rear'd by many a toilsome day,
> By taste like yours approved can ne'er decay.[33]

Later, however, the theatre was found to be structurally defective and, as was stated previously, it suffered general neglect. Another new theatre was therefore decided upon, to which men like Samuel McTier, John Sinclair and Henry Joy subscribed one hundred pounds each for 'silver tickets of admission'.[34] This building was of a very different nature to that which had gone before. It had an excellent location at Arthur Street, was of a good size and had separate entrances for box and pit audiences, with eight dressing rooms and a large green. The *Northern Star* described it thus:

> 'The front of the Theatre facing Ann Street is in length sixty feet, and the side or depth of it in Castle Lane is eighty five. The approaches to it every way are extremely convenient for carriages, and the several entrances for the audiences and actors are well contrived... the people will not in the least incommode each other. The amphitheatre... is laid out with great taste and judgement. It forms a perfect semi–circle, and so contrived that from the very last or uppermost seat of the gallery, the spectator has as good a view as from the front of the boxes or pit. The boxes are roomy and comfortable, and the geometrical staircases to the lattices or upper boxes are very handsome and convenient... The stage is large and great taste has been displayed in the erection of the scenery; and when the house is lighted (which we hear will be done by glass lustres) it must have a most elegant and brilliant effect.'[35]

This theatre opened on February 25, 1793, with what Bernard describes as 'perhaps the most brilliant'[36] audience the Belfast theatre had yet seen.

'Guarded by the brave Belfast volunteers...'

Another audience member, Mrs. McTier, disputes Bernard's account of the opening of the new theatre. In a letter to Doctor William Drennan in

Dublin, she records an occasion marred slightly by political tension, when she

'sat in the box with three officers at the opening of our elegant new theatre on Monday, who appeared as if they were sent to Coventry. God Save the King was the first tune. The officers clapped, *all* the house did the same, but the gallery and a few voices in the pit for the second music called *Ça Ira*, this was silenced and they contented themselves with obtaining and clapping the *Vol[untee]r March*... The gallery indeed growled during the night, but after the play a few gentlemen went up and sat, and all was quiet...'[37]

As the most public of the artforms, theatre would of necessity have been affected by changes in the prevailing social and political climate. Initially, however, such changes were not unfavourable to the theatre in Ulster. At a time of great military fervour, the new volunteer movement was, Lawrence believes, 'very helpful to theatricals'[38]; Clark states that 'the nationalistic cause had now invaded Belfast's theatricals to a far greater extent than anywhere else outside Dublin'.[39] From the first, there appears to have been good relations betwen the Volunteers and the theatre. Formed in 1778, the Belfast Volunteers were praised in an address made at the opening of the Ann Street playhouse on October 23, 1778. The theatre, it was stated, could

'....moor in safety at Belfast,
Where she no storms need dread; nor privateers,
Nor plunderhands of treach'rous Monsieurs,
While guarded by the brave Belfast volunteers.'[40]

Hence, on November 4, 1779 *Tamerlane* was 'performed by desire of the newly enrolled local Volunteers'[41] on the anniversary of the birth of William III, while Sheridan's military piece, *The Camp; or a Trip to Cox Heath* was staged on November 26, 1779, 'doubtless put in the bill out of compliment to the Volunteers'.[42] Notices continued to appear on other bills for dramas re-staged 'by desire of the officers'. At a Volunteers Night at the theatre in April, the Captain of the Volunteers was cheered, the aristocracy groaned (together with agents and Hacks) and musicians called upon to play the 'Volunteers March', 'Liberty Hall' and other patriotic airs.[43] Atkins extended his season in 1785 'on account of the great Volunteer review was to take place on 13 and 14 July'[44], and presented *The Recruiting Officer* for this audience. In Londonderry, too, John Bernard states that the Volunteers

'rendered this place very lively, and benefited the Theatre. The 'band' volunteered for our orchestra, and the officers were very regular in their attendance to the boxes.'[45]

Clark notes that the first performance on record at Londonderry's new theatre was a gala night in 1790 for the local Independent Volunteers, who were entertained with Frederick Pilon's *He Would Be a Soldier*.

By the 1790s, however, and just as the new Belfast theatre was being launched, the atmosphere for theatricals became considerably more difficult. Stage performances were suspended in Belfast in March 1793 due to the Government's decision to disarm and disperse the Belfast Volunteers.[46] In April, the theatre re-opened, but presented a drama of a contentious nature with unfortunate consequences. Written by Belfast clergyman the Reverend Doctor Bambridge, *The Guillotine; or the Death of Louis XVI* caused a 'near-riot'[47] in the theatre in May 1793. The manager was later forced to announce that

> 'he has found it indispensable to take the direction of the Orchestra entirely upon himself, insomuch that no tune which is called for, can be played: and he is convinced that the well known candour and good sense of a Belfast audience will excuse this necessity.'[48]

From mid-1796 to December 1799 there are few records of theatrical activity in Belfast. The theatre re-opened briefly at the beginning of 1796, when civil conditions improved temporarily, but it closed again in June. Then, in late 1798 Mrs. McTier wrote to Dr. Drennan that 'Our theatre opens immediately'.[49] However, Clark states that not until December 1799 did the theatre re-open in Belfast. Instead, for much of this period, Atkins and his company remained in Londonderry, which 'by reason of its large garrison and its heavily pro-English sentiment, remained undisturbed during these years.'[50] There, the manager encouraged the patronage of the military by including army members in his casts on occasion.[51] On his return to Belfast, conditions were obviously still sufficiently disturbed for Atkins to announce that 'Boys of any description will not be admitted to the Gallery'.[52] Mrs. McTier also records incidents of rowdyism at this time, which would continue well into the new century. A disrupted, discordant note therefore characterises this fin-de-siecle period for the theatre in Ulster, one very different to the relaxed existence which it had previously enjoyed. The earlier years of the eighteenth century, however, would generally be remembered as a golden period in the theatre in Ulster, when relations between the theatre and the wider community were relaxed and the theatre was a popular form of entertainment.

References

For further information, the reader is referred particularly to the work of two theatre historians, W.J. Lawrence and William Smith Clark. W.J. Lawrence's book *The Annals of the Old Belfast Stage* was prepared for printing in 1896 but never published; a large volume, it gives year-by-year information on the theatre in Belfast from its origins to 1831. A copy is held in the archive.

William Smith Clark's more recent *The Irish Stage in the County Towns, 1729–1800* provides exhaustive detail on the theatre in Ulster. It builds on Lawrence's work on the Belfast theatre, includes chapters on the theatre in Newry and Londonderry, and features useful appendices on eighteenth century plays and performers outside Dublin. Finally, though not of specific reference to the theatre in Ulster, *The Dublin Stage, 1720–1745* by John C. Greene and Gladys L.H. Clark has a detailed introduction which gives general information about companies, music and the season for the eighteenth century period.

The Nineteenth Century

All the accompaniments are objectionable, the hours, the assembly, the excitement...the songs, the dancing, and the levity of conduct and dress of the figurantes...[1]

Introduction

The nineteenth century was not an auspicious time for the theatre in Ulster. Already somewhat bruised from the on-going civil disturbances at the end of the eighteenth century, it was soon to find that early Victorian values had no place for the playhouse. In this at least it was no different to theatre elsewhere in the British Isles, which underwent a profound decline in the nineteenth century, most markedly so in the first half of the period. By the 1840s, the theatre in Ulster had declined almost to the point of collapse; not until the later years of the century would a concerted battle be undertaken to try and re-gain the lost audiences for serious drama. Managers would then discover that the profound damage done to the theatre in the intervening years was extremely grave. Not even the increasingly fashionable status accorded to theatre in London in the late nineteenth century could initially undo the protracted damage done to the artform in Ulster. Only in the early twentieth century did time, together with the concerted effort and considerable financial input of industrious theatre managers, eventually overcome the problematic reputation the theatre had acquired in the 1800s.

The representation of the nineteenth century theatre in the Linen Hall Library archive mirrors the fate of the artform at this time. As the theatre declines, so too does the archival holding. The script collection of the eighteenth century peters out in the early decades of the next century, and there are few handbills or posters for the period 1800–1860. Any material that the Library holds is almost wholly drawn from the Belfast area. Such scarcity of material may explain the general lack of research undertaken into this period of theatre history in Ulster. Nevertheless, the history of the theatre at this time is a complex and interesting one; interconnected to a tremendous degree with the life of the ordinary people, it is worthy of further attention.

The Early Years

The very first decade of the nineteenth century contained in microcosm the problems which would beset the Belfast theatre throughout the Victorian era. The Arthur Street theatre had re-opened in 1799, when it was felt that the civil disturbances had abated somewhat; however, the turbulence of the 1790s continued into the new century, 'though on a reduced scale'.[2] As in the 1790s, many of the disturbances at the theatre were due to the playing of anthems; the tensions these generated is exemplified by an incident in 1800 wherein two officers

'jumped over the box while *God Save the King* was playing and horse-whipped a captain of a ship sitting in the pit with his hat off... The man proves to be a most loyal subject, a stranger here, not, perhaps blessed with a quick ear, and wishing to be amused at a play. He paid for it.'[3]

Similar disturbances are regularly described by local observer Mrs. Martha

McTier in her letters of the early 1800s, when such trouble appears to have been particularly acute. In August 1803, for example, due to civil disturbance, the theatre doors had to be opened at an earlier time of four o'clock in order to finish performances by nine. In 1804 there was a 'great riot in the play-house on Friday about *God Save the King*'[4], while in 1805 a performance was severely interrupted when 'the gallery would have 'P. [atrick's] Day', the box would not...'[5] A few months later, it was reported that

> 'The people at the theatre have now taken it into their heads to make the audience stand up when Patrick's Day is played, and so polite are the times this is complied with...'[6]

Given these disturbances, it is hardly surprising that many people did not want to suffer for their entertainment. Hence, they began to abandon the theatre for other, less controversial, pursuits. McTier refers to balls and reviews held in August 1804, for example, but states that 'no play bespoke... for Cook has played four nights to empty benches.'[7] Theatre advertisements began to carry notes from the theatre manager requesting that ladies 'will be so kind to him as not to make parties on the play nights'[8], while editorials referred to the 'heavy losses which he [manager Atkins] has sustained this season'.[9] Atkins began, in desperation, to hire novelties to attract audiences; in 1803, William Betty (or 'the Young Roscius') appeared at the age of only 11 years, and in 1805 the six-year old Miss Mudie performed tragic roles at the theatre. Even the success of these infant novelties was not enough, however, to render Atkins' business solvent; for the first time in some three decades of theatre management, his problems were proving insurmountable. In 1805, Atkins finally sold his interests in the theatres in Belfast, Newry and Derry to one Thomas Bellamy; in so doing, he was to prove himself most astute. Over the next half-century his successors would be confronted by even greater difficulties, and as early as 1806 Atkins' era was already being remembered as 'the golden days... when we could boast of one [company] equal perhaps to any provincial corps'.[10]

Certainly, Atkins' resignation ended an era of managerial stability for the theatre in Belfast. Bellamy was quickly succeeded by Talbot, who lasted longest after Atkins in managing the theatre between 1809 and 1820. Nevertheless, he faced at times 'nightly disorder', according to Lawrence, and eventually appealed for official protection for the theatre.[11] Such disturbances were, by now, certainly not confined to the political. As elsewhere, general rowdiness had become a feature of the theatre experience and reviews frequently referred, for example, to the 'open impertinence' of audience members towards performers.[12] Hence, despite renovating the building, Talbot too saw houses dwindle and increasingly programmed more populist 'turns' encompassing everything from tight-rope acts and slack-wire exhibitions to Madame Girardelli, the Fire-Proof Lady, and a troop of performing dogs in 1819. The frequency of such acts increased over the years of Talbot's managerial period, while the more well-to-do citizens continued to stay away. The manager pleaded to no avail with the 'Lady Matrons'

'to suspend their evening parties of Wednesdays, leaving one night at least open to the rational pleasure of a well-regulated Theatre, without suffering CARDS to engross the whole.'[13]

Though the fashionable set returned to the theatre for special occasions, they stubbornly refused to do so for regular stock company performances either for Talbot or those who succeeded him. Some eight managers tried their hand at the Belfast theatre over the next decade, each engaging 'an inferior and cheaper stock company' and resorting 'to all sorts of flashy and undignified devices to catch the public.'[14] Hence, in 1842, the then manager Mr. Cunningham ended the season by acknowledging

'the many obligations he is under to those friends who, notwithstanding the blight under which theatricals appear to wither in Belfast, have endeavoured to uphold him in his exertions to cater for public amusement... the management has suffered a heavy pecuniary loss, during this and the former season; still, no efforts have been spared to render the entertainments worthy of public patronage. Tragedy, Comedy, Opera, a mimic Monkey, and, though last, not least, a real ass have all been tried in succession and, excepting in the case of the quadruped, without success...'[15]

It cannot have helped Mr. Cunningham that reviews of the season earlier still spoke of 'scenes of unreasonable clamour' when it was insisted upon that an encore should bear the Irish interpretation of 'a new song'.[16] Even the fact that Cunningham himself conducted his business with complete 'regard to moral respectability and the bienséances'[17] could not attract decent houses to his performances, and for much of the season, as in previous years, it was reported that 'there was scarcely a hand in the house to applaud him.'[18] Though he would manage the theatre again on other occasions, Cunningham would have no more success. The *Northern Whig* worriedly stated that for the town, 'the inference to be deducted from so complete a failure is dispiriting in the extreme'. The drama had, seemingly indefinitely, fallen into 'the sear and yellow leaf',[19] and the future of the theatre, the newspaper concluded, was grim.

Such a serious decline was not, naturally, caused solely by in-house disturbances. Though these significantly launched the theatre in Belfast into the new century on a most uncertain footing, and continued on a sporadic basis, they compounded a trend away from the theatre on a national basis. Many factors were blamed for this decline; it was said theatre was in difficulty because

'star actors received immense salaries and authors not nearly enough; that actors and managers treated authors abominably; that the later dinner hour kept fashionable people away; that such people did not attend theatres because the lower classes were too noisily in evidence; that anyway they preferred exhibiting themselves at the opera and at the visits of

French companies; that the solid middle class did not come because of increased evangelical hostility to the theatre and because of the presence of their inferiors who corrupted the drama because they did come and liked mere entertainment and vulgar show;... that too many new amusements were competing for public attention; that people preferred reading novels to going to plays...[20] [that] the theatre for them simply became unfashionable.'[21]

Many of these factors are attributable, directly or indirectly, to the tremendous social upheaval occurring in society at this time. Massive population shifts became a major feature of Belfast history as early as the first decade of the nineteenth century. The town's population increased by an astonishing 47% between 1801 and 1811, growing from 19,000 to 27,832 in just one decade. In 1821 the population had reached 37,277, and just ten years later it was at 53,287. By 1841 the population stood at 70,447.[22] As with the other rapidly developing industrial towns, this massive influx placed tremendous strain on the sleepy market town that had formerly been Belfast. Jonathan Bardon states that 'The passions of the Ulster countryside were imported into Belfast with far-reaching consequences'[23]; given the vulnerability of theatre to social stresses, this would prove particularly true for the artform. Societal movements in two distinct directions were to leave the theatre struggling in a vacuum, and finding a formula to satisfy both middle-class mores and working-class demands became the chief concern of the nineteenth century theatre manager.

Such a formula could hardly emerge with ease. Certainly, on the one hand, the potential audience for theatre was ever-increasing, and with it the possibilities for profit. Hence, despite the considerable risk, the succession of entrepreneurs prepared to attempt the business of theatre management. On the other hand, however, the nature of that potential audience elicited numerous problems. Given the on-going nature of nineteenth century immigration, every manager was regularly confronted with an entirely new audience unfamiliar to theatre. Arriving in unmeasured proportions from the countryside, many immigrants sought work in the new industries, particularly textiles, and managed with difficulty to make a living. Working long hours, and lacking much disposable income, this new urban labour force constituted an unlikely audience for the theatre in its contemporary state. The playhouse they met on arrival was in decline, no longer a focal point of the town's social life. Its repertory was not aimed at their needs, but had historically developed to suit a relatively literate community with sufficient leisure time to spend several hours on a weekday evening at a theatre. The prices charged by the theatre were also an issue. It is telling that as the century progressed, admission prices remained stable or were actually reduced. In 1806, for example, the Lower Boxes cost 4/4, Upper Boxes 3/3, Pit 2/2 and the Gallery 1/1.[24] By 1817, over a decade later, a theatre seat now cost 4/2 in the Lower Boxes, while Upper Boxes cost 3/4, the Pit 2/1, and the Gallery 1/3.[25] In 1826 the Lower Boxes had been further reduced to 4/-, with the Upper Boxes costing 3/-, Pit 2/- and Gallery 1/-.[26] By the 1840s, prices had plummeted. The Lower Boxes had fallen by almost a third their price in 1806 to 3/-; the Upper Boxes were now 2/- and the Pit and Gallery 1/6 and 6d respectively. The fall in prices may of course be attributed to the unpopularity of the theatre, but must also have been prompted to suit audience requirements. Even these relatively stable prices were beyond the reaches of the poorest labourers; to a weaver earning twelve to fifteen shillings in 1811 one shilling for a gallery seat represented a considerable outlay. Though somewhat more affordable for a spinner, who earned £2.7s weekly,[27] it would only constitute money and time well spent if the entertainment provided was relevant in some way to his or her own existence. If it was not, why then attend the offerings of the (often cold and damp) playhouse? And if one did invest hard-earned money and time at the theatre, then why not indulge the few brief hours of a performance in 'talking, laughing (but not at the stage), flirting, eating, drinking, walking about, condemning and praising with equal vociferousness, inattention, and a dozen other practices...'?[28]

To this for many years the theatre aimlessly sought a response. In part, this was because its existence was considerably constrained. This is exemplified by the case of one manager Mason, who decided in 1820 to overtly appeal to the working classes. Organising performances on Saturday nights to better suit their needs, his efforts were met with considerable criticism. The *Belfast News-Letter* queried 'Whether the practice of playing on Saturday night, which is novel, is advisable? Certainly it is disapproved of by many well-meaning inhabitants.'[29] The practice was soon discontinued, and Mason disappeared after a season, but not before being complimented for his

'attention to the interest of decency and morals, by excluding those indelicate phrases which so often sully the pages of our immortal bard, and of many minor dramatists, without improving the interest of the scene. It is hoped the Manager will extend his attention to this point, through the entire performances on his stage.'[30]

The theatre, as with much else, was already being encompassed by the complex cocktail of the religious and the social which comprised early Victorian values. It is a given that this was an essentially religious age, in the sense that

'Protestant evangelicalism was a basic ingredient in the dominant ideology... Men's values and standards, their assumptions and attitudes, functioned within this context. Religion as a social force operated at a number of different levels.'[31]

In Ulster specifically, though the actual 'number of adherents to a committed evangelical life-style was always a minority in terms of percentage of population, its social code penetrated deep into Ulster culture.'[32] This code emphatically did not include theatre. An 1837 publication, *Lectures and Conversations on the Theatre*, succinctly outlines the standard reasons for disdain for the theatre, rhetorically asking 'if attending the entertainments of the stage be an unnecessary and unprofitable expense, and a foolish and unjustifiable waste of time...;– if such entertainments have a great tendency to promote vice and profaneness, are offensive to a modest ear, and irreconcilable to Christian piety:– if they are pleasing only to corrupt nature, to the unrenewed and unsanctified part in man...:– if they do greatly indispose people for the devotion of the closet, the family, and the House of God, spoiling their taste for spiritual enjoyments, and disposition for religious exercises:–... in a word, if they are amusements that are unsuitable and unbecoming the character of persons professing godliness... then we must pronounce them vain, impure and destructive.'[33]

Such fierce attacks were echoed by the clergy of Belfast when they began to address the task of moral reform. John Gray notes incidents of specific religious opposition in the 1840s which were to prove 'lasting and acutely damaging'[34] to the theatre; similarly, David Hempton and Myrtle Hill instance the energetic rejection of Thomas Drew, who in an appeal to the press declared that drama was

'the most dangerous part of our literature. Throughout the entire range of all plays an anti-Christian principle is maintained... when these writings are transferred to the stage there, indeed, do our objections become stronger a thousand fold. All the accompaniments are objectionable, the hours, the assembly, the excitement, the base language of the profligate portion of the audience, the indecent exposure of the persons called fashionable, the songs, the dancing, and the levity of conduct and dress of the figurantes... How few escape privation and sin?'[35]

This letter was signed by every clergyman of the established church in Belfast. They would, most likely, have willingly accepted Thackeray's accusation in the 1840s that they were single-handedly to blame for the state of the 'poor neglected dramatic Muse of Ulster'.[36] However, it would probably be fairer to say, as do Hempton and Hill, that a complex interaction took place between belief and practice in the nineteenth century. As a consequence, a mutual reinforcement occurred between religion and the 'respectability' which became a 'central feature in Protestant culture'.[37] Of this, the theatre became a casualty.

In the face of such hostility, it is hardly surprising that the average theatre manager felt unwilling to undertake controversial programming. Like Mason, many inclined instead towards self-censorship of the material presented, and indeed, the innately conservative middle class demanded, as has been seen, to be so protected. However, working class taste was 'indifferent to... static poetic tragedy, genteel comic wit, and delicate sentimentality'[38] and sought instead new forms, such as the melodrama, which had robust energy and spectacle at their core. The consequent dilemma at grass-roots is obvious. Though polite taste dominated society generally, and kept a sharp eye on the theatre, the respectable citizen steadfastly refused to attend the playhouse. Conversely, those whom Thackeray did find in the Belfast theatre, the gallery denizens who 'stamped, and stormed, and shouted and clapped... with roars of delight'[39], would not be content with classical drama. The Belfast theatre manager therefore attempted to tread carefully between the two, keeping within the boundaries of middle class taste, but attempting simultaneously to satisfy the new audiences. However, the limbo-like existence which resulted left the playhouse benches at the Arthur Street theatre only sparsely populated. Not until the last three decades of the nineteenth century would change come about; when it did, a slow, difficult and costly process commenced which testified to the extent of the theatre's previous decline.

1850–1900

The mid-nineteenth century saw the first deliberate attempts in London to bring the moneyed and educated classes back to the theatre. This began initially through the efforts of certain theatre managers, most notably Samuel Phelps at Sadler's Wells Theatre from 1844–1862. However, it was Charles Kean's management of the Princess's Theatre from 1850–1859 which, Michael Booth believes, marked the turn of the theatrical tide.[40] This in turn was extended by the success of the Bancrofts in the 1860s in attracting society to the Prince of Wales' theatre, so that by the latter end of the century the theatre was again fashionable and respectable in the metropolis. This success was attributed to many factors, but initially at least, Royal support was of tremendous assistance. Queen Victoria regularly attended plays, and 'what the queen thought significant, society valued and the church commended.'[41] Hence audiences began to grow in size and increase in respectability, cautiously beginning to return to the comfortable Bancrofts' theatre which featured curtains, carpets and white lace antimacassars on seats.[42] Significantly, comfortable orchestra stalls also began to replace the pit, whose former occupants were now confined to an area which was 'airless, dark and badly sighted under the low overhand of the first balcony'.[43] As these orchestra stalls were more expensive than the pit had been, the former 'pittites' were reduced in number and audience behaviour began to improve. So too did audience figures, as with the development of new railway systems, those from the provinces could also consider visiting the theatre more regularly. Meanwhile, the music halls had begun to siphon the working and middle class audiences from the theatre[44], leaving the way free for the domination of middle class tastes. As polite society returned to the theatre, plays and performances followed to suit. Domestic copyright protection increased, and successful playwrights were offered new percentage systems of royalties, ensuring the return of writers to the artform. They began to write for the well-heeled stalls audiences rather than the noisy and enthusiastic pittites, and the plays which resulted showed considerable evidence of the 'engulfing flood of domestic taste'[45]. Styles of acting were consequently also refined and toned down. Hence, by the pre-war years of the twentieth century, the London theatre was finally prospering, having been transformed into a middle class theatre, with a middle class audience and a middle class drama.[46]

Despite a lively general interest in the affairs of the metropolis, Belfast was very slow to follow these theatrical developments in London. Not until the 1870s did the first efforts to regain the fashionable audience for the playhouse occur, and even then the audience take-up was not as swift. However, patient work and astute management from the manager of the Theatre Royal, J.F. Warden, slowly began to woo the well-to-do back to the theatre. Having taken the Theatre Royal over in 1864, Warden demolished the 78 year old building in 1871 and erected instead the New or Second Theatre Royal on the same site. This was a sumptuous building, far grander than that which had preceded it and able to accommodate over two thousand people – twice as many as the original. The building was thus designed with an eye to the continuing flood of immigrants to Belfast. From a population of 70,000 in 1841, the figures had swelled to 87,062 in 1851; in 1861 they stood at 121,602 and in 1871, the year of the theatre's opening, Belfast contained 174,412 inhabitants.[47] Even allowing for a boundary extension in 1852, this represented extraordinarily rapid growth which Warden fully intended to exploit. His grand edifice was the first step in so doing; the next was careful programming developed through long-standing experience of local taste. In this, the manager was encouraged by two developments: the arrival of the music-hall to Belfast, and the development of massive touring companies from the metropolis which the new building could now accommodate.

The first Belfast music-hall, The Alhambra, opened at North Street in 1873 under the management of Dan Lowrey. A centre for working-class entertainment, it was an extension of the singing saloons which had existed previously in what was now effectively a city. The music hall's 'sentimentality, domesticity, patriotism and completely satisfying light entertainment'[48] attracted large numbers, and its relaxed nature met with considerable approval. One Belfast critic explained

'there is more freedom in the halls; one can saunter here and there in easy fashion, your journey being unheeded by the audience, while in a theatre if you only cough the respectable (sic) and straight-laced audience stare you out of countenance; and should you be intrepid enough to leave your seat to gargle your throat, you do so at the risk of muttered imprecations from the self-same respectable and straight-laced crowd.'[49]

When the Alhambra was advertised as for sale on November 2, 1900, it was stated that it had five bars and a 2,000 seat capacity. Simultaneous with its development, the Theatre Royal was undergoing a considerable shift in emphasis. The *Belfast News-Letter* theatre columnist in 1882 noted

'the very important and palpable fact that a stock company at the [Theatre] Royal is a thing of the past...With perhaps one or two exception there is no theatre in the United Kingdom which now maintains a stock company, the task of upholding the drama devolving at the present time upon travelling companies, organised for the express purposes of rendering with – in most instances – efficiency, special plays.'[50]

Even by the standards of today, these travelling companies were enormous. Managers such as Fred Mouillot had at least a dozen companies on the road, employing on occasion 'the big total of 600'.[51] The Belfast periodical *Nomad's Weekly* estimated that the average 'No. 1' company of a typical show would travel for 30 or 40 weeks at a time 'with as many as 70 or 80 people'.[52] For special shows, companies of 100 or more could be appointed, and would undertake gruelling schedules which made full use of the relatively new methods of rail and sea transport. In 1902, for example, the first week of Sarah Bernhardt's July tour took her on Sunday to London, Monday to Dublin, Tuesday to Belfast, Wednesday to Glasgow, Thursday to Edinburgh, Friday to Newcastle, to Liverpool on Saturday, and to Manchester on Monday.[53] In general, travelling companies brought versions of London successes to the provinces. This meant the demise of any local contact with what was being performed. However, as John Gray points out, the increasing popularity of the travelling companies helped to reduce objections on moral grounds as 'local doubters could be assured that the English bourgeoisie had seen and approved of it first'.[54] Together with the establishment of the music-hall, this meant conditions were more favourable for the theatre in Belfast than previously. Little by little, Warden weaned his fledgling Theatre Royal audience on a mix of opera, pantomime, musical comedy, society drama and occasional visits from star performers such as Barry Sullivan or Irving. Some of the well-to-do began to return on a regular basis for visits by such opera companies as the Carl Rosa Opera or the D'Oyly Carte; eventually, audiences on such occasions even became fashionable. However, the extent of their cross-over to drama is difficult to establish, particularly as disturbances continued at the theatre into the 1880s. These were evidently substantial enough for *The Belfast Morning News* to note in 1886 that 'special provision has been made for the suppression of these vexatious displays'[55]; despite this, the police were still required on occasion.

It is hardly surprising then that in the 1890s, when Warden decided to begin a concerted campaign to woo the middle and upper classes back to the theatre, he chose not to do so at the Theatre Royal. Through longevity, the Theatre Royal was ineradicably associated with the public dis-approbation which had greeted theatre throughout the nineteenth century. A new building with no such problematic history, promoted from the first as the most respectable of establishments, would have a better chance of success. Hence, on December 23, 1895, the new Grand Opera House and Cirque opened on the site of Ginett's Circus in Glengall Street. This was a most imposing structure designed by theatre architect Frank Matcham, and deliberately promoted to attract the moneyed classes. Seating 2,500 people, its boxes had 'elegant silk plush draperies and the floors are covered with thick carpets...'[56]; reports speak of 'polished marble', of 'rich open work scrolled design', of 'massive richly decorated columns',[57] of 'an imposing centre facade, flanked with square towers, crowned with boldly moulded and domed minarets...',[58] of handsome upholstery and velvet covered seats 'divided with brass arms'.[59] As a consequence, however, the status of the Theatre Royal was now rather vague. Given the success of some newly established and more respectable music halls such as the Empire or the Olympia Palace, Warden might have chosen to re-dedicate the Royal to variety and open it to the masses. However, he did not do so. For his new and considerably risky venture to succeed, the manager needed to sustain a respectable reputation for theatre generally. The Theatre Royal had been the 'Establishment' theatre of Belfast for over a century; there had begun the process of encouraging the city's *hoi-polloi* back to the theatre, albeit for opera. Hence, Warden seems to have deliberately blurred the relationship between the two 'legitimate' theatres, and no strict demarcation was made initially between them.

Within three years, however, the new theatre was beginning to flounder. After an initial honeymoon period, the Grand Opera House experienced considerable difficulty in winning over its prospective audience. Warden, with his long experience of programming to suit local tastes, died in 1898 and it was left to his son, Fred, to manage the two theatres. He soon came under sustained attack from local periodicals such as *The Magpie* where writers established their argument against him on the basis of taste. Commentators stated repeatedly that Belfast was now a major city, of some standing and reputation. Its people, they thought, deserved the very best the theatre had to offer, and would respond appropriately once proper provisions were made for its new sophistication. However, Warden had, it was concluded, poor managerial ability and programmed second- or even third-rate companies much of the time at the two theatres. Hence he had, they believed, doomed Belfast's theatrical standard to 'an exceedingly low one on the average'.[60] Not surprisingly, annual takings for the two theatres fell, particularly after an unsuccessful experiment in restoring the stock company at the Theatre Royal in 1899. Hence, in 1901, the directors of Warden Limited announced that prices at the Theatre Royal were being slashed, in the hope that an

> experiment of running the Theatre Royal on 'popular lines' might act as an inducement to our working classes to become more liberal patrons of the drama in Belfast than is at present the case... The new [price] scale will, we believe, bring theatre-going within the reach of the purse of the most humble members of the community.

The working classes were already 'patrons of the drama'; time and again contemporary reviewers had pointed out that when the more expensive areas of the Grand Opera House were empty, it was the 'popular parts of the house that are best patronised'.[61] Warden's announcement was therefore most likely intended to reassure the 'people of position and wealth'[62] in the city about his new theatre. His statement distinguished clearly and publicly between the Grand Opera House and the Theatre Royal; if the latter was now intended for the working classes, then the respectable could confidently expect the Grand Opera House to be reserved solely for their use. Immediately after so designating his buildings on class grounds, Warden responded directly to his band of critics. For 1901 he programmed the very finest companies available from the metropolis, including many of the names mentioned as being suited to Belfast's newly refined tastes.

Surely now the theatre would attract the polite and fashionable of Belfast?

Warden's experiment was a disaster. The Grand Opera House audience proved extraordinarily erratic, and it rapidly became clear that success in London was no guarantee of a good attendance in Belfast. Houses for the famed Sir Herbert Beerbohm Tree were 'disappointing'.[63] Forbes Robinson's company was 'anything but adequately supported'[64]; George Alexander and Mrs. Langtry had small attendances. Conversely, Ellen Terry and Sir Henry Irving had full houses 'in every part'.[65] Mr. Fred Mouillot, a member of Warden Ltd., attributed this to natural caution on the part of audiences:

> 'a curious thing I have noticed about the Belfast public is that they seem very frightened of going to anything at first, For instance, when 'Sweet Nell of Old Drury' was here, with Fred Terry and Julia Neilson, they were very slow in going at the beginning, although these artistes are among the best known of the present day.'[66]

Hence, leadership became an issue. However, the attitude both of society leaders and of the religious to theatre at this time seems to have been marginally less clear-cut than was the case previously. A letter to the *Ireland's Saturday Night* newspaper from 'A Stage Lover', for example, exemplifies one contemporary Christian attitude; rather than reject the theatre outright, it is asked: 'Why cannot we have a theatre run on religious lines? ...We certainly want a Christianity which will redeem the stage and purify it.'[67] Likewise, at the Church Conference at Armagh in September 1892, one Colonel Burges, a keynote speaker on 'How to Deepen Interest in the Services of Our Church', proposed that clergymen would never

> 'be really effective, either in the prayer-desk or in the pulpit, until you have in you something of the *Actor!* Do not be shocked, I implore you, and do not misunderstand me, for there are actors and actors!... [the inspired actor] throws himself into his part with such an earnestness that he feels every word that he utters to his heart's core, and electrifies his audience with the intensity of his emotion.'[68]

That Burges hoped those around him would 'not be scandalised' indicates the daring of the statement; that the statement was made at all, however, is notable. It suggests that change, if barely perceptible, was occurring; this may also be gleaned from the general absence, rather than presence, of comments in relation to theatre at this time. It would be wrong to make too much of this; the Christian 'Stage Lover' did not, for example, feel sufficiently confident to publicly attach a name to his or her letter. One might simply say that where previously there had been blanket opposition, now there was for some at least a question mark. How, then, to gauge which of the forthcoming attractions would be deemed acceptable? Who would be deemed an *Actor*, by Burges' standards? And for what reasons?

Fred Warden chose to focus on precisely this ambiguity, rather than the issues of taste beloved of the press, in his public announcements. When appealing for public support, Warden Ltd. fore-grounded arguments about morality, and embarked on a steadfast campaign to counteract connections between immorality and the theatre. The theatre, Warden declared time and again, had changed for the better:

> 'The power of the stage for good is universally admitted. It possesses a refining and educational influence that cannot be over-estimated. The theatre is not merely a commercial undertaking pure and simple but has become in these days a distinct part of our social and educational system...'[70]

Other statements which followed were in a similar vein: the theatre was not a wicked place; actors and actresses led the quietest and most self-denying lives; in their hearts people loved the true drama. Given time for re-gaining audiences and building loyalty, such an approach might have worked. Time, however, was not allowed. As the argument for theatre had been publicly whipped up on the issue of taste, every rejection of a visiting theatre company became something more, a further indication that Belfast was not in fact a city of discernment. Even minor failures were accorded a significance that it is doubtful they warranted. 'It must simply mean a want of culture', the local press concluded; 'Belfast in its relations to theatrical affairs is a city by itself.'[71] Coming after a half-century of theatrical neglect by the city, this was to prove most unfortunate. Though Belfast had been by no means unique in its rejection of the theatre in the first half of the 1800s, commentators had designated it so. Now, this 'unique' rejection was being compounded at a time when both London and Dublin were welcoming the artform back to respectable society. Belfast thus took itself to be an 'icy' place for theatre, a disastrous place to play, uniquely philistine. The general local consensus was now to abandon the attempt at culture, accept the fact that Belfast was a purely industrial city, and see the Opera House as a failed experiment. The Grand Opera House closed as a serious theatre in 1904, and became instead the Palace of Varieties, a music-hall for the masses; legitimate drama trudged back once again to the smaller Theatre Royal. The theatrical experiment had failed; Belfast's relationship with the legitimate theatre had suffered its first defeat of the new century.

The theatrical war, however, was far from over. The nine-year battle for the Grand Opera House left an unfortunate short-term legacy. Belfast's reputation and standing among the wider artistic community was shattered, with some touring companies and artists temporarily refusing to play in the city. The tentative confidence accorded the theatre by a small number of leading members of respectable society had been very publicly deflated. The taint of immorality had not been overcome, and had perhaps even been reinforced, by the theatre's closure for legitimate drama. And an unsure city embarking on one of its first tentative cultural advances had had to abandon the project and internalise the term 'philistine'. In hindsight, the city was in many ways a victim of its own expectations. The 'hint of strain'[72] Jonathan Bardon detects in Belfast's boasting at the turn of the century is certainly detectable in its early twentieth century theatre history. In a dash to prove that 'the taste of the Belfast audiences still remains at a high level' *Belfast Critic*, November 3, 1900, p. 153, equivalent to that of London, the extremely chequered career of the theatre in the nineteenth century was ignored; too little attention was paid to the broader local factors, and the theatre suffered greatly as a result. The timing of Warden Ltd. may also have been an underlying problem. By launching his new experiment at a time of social change, J.F. Warden may have hoped to influence favourably the direction such change would take. In practice, this did not happen. Instead, the legitimate theatre in Belfast ended the nineteenth century somewhat defeated. Perhaps most shocking was the fact that the theatrical link with London had been firmly and most publicly interrogated. In this, the initial Grand Opera House failure was significant. The theatre landscape had been notably altered; former cultural certainties could no longer be relied upon. As a consequence of its Grand Opera House experience, the theatre in Belfast entered the new century unwillingly confronted by niggling questions of local identity. The twentieth century keynote was thereby struck, and a glimpse provided of issues for the theatre in the future.

Late Victorian and Edwardian Theatres

'Miss Carson was of opinion that they should not train up the children of the house
to go to theatre. The Chairman – Miss Carson, my own children go there.'[1]
– Belfast Board of Guardians Report, 1900

Theatre Royal, Belfast (1871–1915)

The first Theatre Royal closed in March 1871 when J.F. Warden, the manager, decided a grander theatre was needed to suit the rapidly expanding Belfast population.[2] The old building, which had originally been built in 1793, was 'not much to boast of' in its later years, and visitors reported being struck by its general 'inferiority'.[3] Hence it was rapidly demolished, and work commenced at breathtaking speed on the new construction. By September 1871 the new Theatre Royal was ready for opening. Its six month construction period was quite astonishing when the scale of this 'heavy arcaded four-storey building'[4], is considered:

'There are two fronts: one – the principal one – in Arthur Square, and another in Castle Lane. The former measures sixty-feet, and the latter has a street frontage of one hundred and seven feet... The Arthur Square elevation is about eighty feet high... The house is built entirely of brick, with stone dressings... The public entrances – four in number – are each six feet wide... The stairs are of Riga oak... The stage and its entire fittings are the work of Mr. J.R. Chapman, a gentleman who has fitted up stages in some of the best theatres in London and the provinces. It has cost Mr. Warden close on £1000... From the footlights to the back wall it measures forty-one feet. The entire breadth is fifty-six feet, with a proscenium opening of twenty-six feet by twenty-eight feet... At one side of the stage, immediately at the footlights, is a large brass plate on which are sixteen gas taps with handles. From this point the gas can be turned off or on in any part of the house, or all the house... There are four wings on each side, thus making five entrances to the stage: and at the extreme back, in the Castle-lane side, is a large door, over which is a pulley for the purpose of lifting and taking in scenery, luggage, &c... Beneath the stage, on the Castle-lane side, are the band, ballet and supers' rooms... The 'stars' room is fitted up with drawers and benches round the walls, and is supplied with a basin and two pipes for hot and cold water... The wardrobe is lighted from Castle-lane, and fitted up with sixteen presses, in each of which there are three shelves. Higher up on the same side is a property-room, and above all, high up over the pit and stage, are the painting-room, carpenters' shop and what is known as the 'gridiron'. On the very top of the house, immediately above the stage, a large tank is placed; it is estimated to hold about two thousand gallons of water... The new Royal is estimated to hold two thousand two hundred people – twice as many as the old house was able to accommodate... the theatre lavatories and retiring-rooms are in abundance... The ceiling is a perfect gem. There is a large sunlight in the centre, and from it there radiate eleven panels... They represent architecture, astronomy, comedy, dancing, eloquence, history, music. memory, painting and tragedy...'[5]

This new Theatre Royal, evidently intended to attract a more well-to-do audience than its predecessor, opened with a production of Douglas Jarrold's comedy, *Time Works Wonders*. Italian opera followed, and a *Belfast News-Letter* piece in 1881 commented:

> 'Many a time and oft the walls have resounded with the glorious strains of Mozart and Rossinin, the airs of Verdi and Bellini... High life, low life in all its phases have been represented. The occupants of the auditorium have in turn been roused to indignation and passion at the villanies of Richard or Iago, to horror at the treachery of Macbeth... have heard the story of Claude Melnotte's love, and traced the diplomacy of a Richelieu. And in later days crowded houses have testified to the popularity of *The Bells of Corneville* and *The Pinafore*. The triumphs of Sullivan, Irving, Toole and all the rest of the leaders of the profession will have lasting places in the memories of those for whom Mr. Warden has catered so long and so well... [he] enjoyed in no small measure the confidence of the public.[6]

This account, unfortunately, was written on the occasion of the theatre's near-complete destruction. Despite the built-in safety precautions, the theatre was burnt out in 1881. After the fire on June 8, 'four bare and lofty walls, some tottering pillars, a few blackened beams' were all that was left.[7] Almost immediately, Warden set about re-building the theatre. English theatre architect C.J. Phipps arrived to supervise the process, and the contractors finished the task in just thirteen weeks. By December 22, 1881 the new theatre was ready for opening; contemporary descriptions were most complimentary:

> 'The appearance of the new theatre from the auditorium is extremely handsome: the decorations are light, and in keeping with modern taste, elaborate carving being substituted in many parts for the ordinary effect of superficial gilding, and the general tone of the walls and the upholstery being in every way subdued... the new building is, indeed, a model theatre.[8]

On the opening night Barry Sullivan presented Lord Lytton's comedy, *Money*. Warden then made a speech, and announced the programme for the season. This, a strong programme, consisted of Mr. Joseph Eldred's Comedy Opera Company; Adeline Stanhope's company; Edward Compton and his Old English Comedy Company; the annual pantomime; the first Belfast appearance of Miss Mari Majilton; the Carl Rosa Opera Company; the London comedy, *Imprudence*; Edgar Bruce and Company with 'the aesthetic comedy of *The Colonel*'; and finally Mr. Edward Terry. Some of these companies would return regularly: the annual visits of the Carl Rosa and D'Oyly Carte Opera Companies were always very well attended, and companies such as that of Edward Compton or F.R. Benson were favourites in a place 'noted for fierce loyalties rather than any particular taste'.[9] Such companies offered an astonishing range of shows in the course of their short visits; between January 21 and 30, 1889, for example, Compton's company presented *Davy Garrick, Twelfth Night, The Honeymoon, Road to Ruin, School for Scandal,* and *The Liar and the Critic*. Melodrama was a favourite in Belfast, as elsewhere, at this time. The nature of the shows presented can be imagined from the programme description of *The Eviction*, presented by Frank O'Grady's Company. Characters included Lord Hardman, the landlord, his daughter Lady Eveleen, 'handsome, high-minded and outspoken – the friend of the poor', and Dermot McMahon, 'an intelligent Irish lad... open as the day, the index of a noble and generous heart'. Another high-point of the Theatre Royal's year was the Warden Easter Pantomime. In March 1888 this was *The Fair One With the Golden Locks*; featuring the Yokohama Troupe, the Bale Bicycle Troupe, and 'Tregatour with his shadow graph', it had a then lengthy run of three weeks.

Heartened by the popularity of the Theatre Royal, and with an eye to the ever-increasing Belfast population, Warden decided to expand his operations at the turn of the century. Hence, he opened the Grand Opera House, Belfast in 1895, and operated the two theatres in tandem for a number of years. In time, however, it became evident that the Grand Opera House was finding difficulty in winning over its prospective audience. Hence, in an attempt to firmly establish the new venture, prices at the Theatre Royal were substantially reduced, 'leaving the Grand Opera House as the implied destination for quality'[10] and the Royal the location for the popular end of the market. Despite this, Opera House audiences proved as erratic as ever, and particularly so for the expensive London companies they had been relied on to support. Meanwhile, the cheaper seats in the house were very well patronised on these occasions. Hence, in 1903, and in the face of a highly critical press, Fred Warden, successor to his father, announced that the Grand Opera House would become a Palace of Varieties, while the smaller

> 'Arthur Square Theatre passes into the hands of the upholsterer and refurnisher, to reappear in all the new glories of Belfast's only legitimate theatre. The renovation process will mean the expenditure of a cool thousand pounds... improvements include the conversion of the pit into a modern parterre, fitted up with all the latest in tip-up chairs, which can be booked at a florin... in lieu of their beloved pit the present day patrons of this part of the house will find themselves translated aloft to the upper circle for their popular 'bob'.'[11]

The Grand Opera House opened as the Palace of Varieties on February 1, 1904 on the basis of two performances nightly, at 7 and 9 pm. The Theatre Royal, now deemed 'a magnificent house...tho' the price has been doubled'[12], opened on January 30, 1904. It remained the home of serious drama in Belfast until 1909, when the Grand Opera resumed its old title and increased its prices. Once again, ticket prices at the Theatre Royal plummeted; the first presentation under the revised system, *How Girls Are Brought to Ruin*, set the keynote for the 'New Sensational Drama'[13] to come. However, the theatre faced competition from the cinema, now the newer, more popular entertainment. In 1915 it was announced that

> 'The progress and popularity of the cinematograph have induced Messrs. Warden Ltd. to embark on a fresh venture, and a result of this they

have resolved to raze the Theatre Royal to the ground, and to erect in its place a stately and commodious picture house...'[14]

The final performance at Belfast's Theatre Royal took place on March 10, 1915, with a benefit for the members of the staff. Artists from the Royal Hippodrome, Empire, Alhambra and Coliseum participated, and 'standing room was at a premium'[15] for the final show. The building was subsequently demolished, and a cinema built on its site. This, the Royal Cinema, opened on December 16, 1916, and had a capacity audience of 1,000 for its first film, *The Misleading Lady*. The Royal Cinema became 'one of *the* cinemas to frequent',[16] and in the 'lean years between the wars it was this cinema, together with the assured success of the annual pantomime, that helped... keep the Opera House going.'[17] However, the Royal Cinema could not compete with the circuit cinemas in the 1960s. It was in turn finally demolished in 1961.

Empire Theatre, Belfast (1894–1961)
The Empire Players / Belfast Repertory Company

On December 3, 1894 the Empire Theatre of Varieties opened under the ownership of Adam Findlater. Traditionally associated with singing saloon entertainment, its site at Victoria Square had previously been occupied by the Buffalo, the New Colosseum, and Traverse's Musical Theatre. Now, however, the venue was intended to attract 'an entirely new audience. For the first time, women could attend without fear of reproach, and the lavish interior overcame the qualms of the business classes.'[18] A two-hour 'private view' of the theatre was provided in advance of the opening to some three hundred of the commercial and professional classes of the city, and the *Belfast News-Letter* sternly concluded that

> 'Modernity characterises the building and its equipment... we have no doubt the theatre will pay its way, an important consideration for the proprietors, who cannot be expected to afford amusement on the philanthropic basis.'[19]

The Empire offered seats at 'popular prices' ranging from 3d to 1s 6d, on a 'no-money returned'[20] basis. Initially, however, the music-hall encountered difficulties. Audiences varied according to the quality of the 'turns' provided; 'fairly large' houses were noted in reviews, but so too were periodic complaints about the rather average quality of the entertainments provided. Hence, for example, in February 1898 one surprised reviewer described a programme of good quality, 'far superior to any compiled for several months past',[21] while the appointment of a new manager, Mr. Con Salmon would, it was hoped, 'rapidly work the Empire up to that position which it should occupy by virtue of its comfort and location.'[22] Occasional reports of rowdyism at the theatre cannot have helped; in one account a Miss Walker, 'possessor of a cultivated voice', was 'interrupted and interfered with in a manner which reflects the utmost discredit upon one part of the house, and one felt inclined to wish that a professional pugilist had been engaged to put a stop to the disgraceful conduct of those who were unable to appreciate her cultured vocalism.'[23]

It would be unfair to characterise the Empire audiences entirely from such accounts, and such occurrences are not commonly referred to in reviews of the early Empire shows. Nevertheless, even irregular incidents of this kind cannot have been welcomed by a newly established music-hall, particularly at a time of extreme sensitivity regarding respectability. There were also reports that the stage could not be seen from various vantage points, and that the building, while beautiful, was badly designed and needed adjustments.[24]

Given such difficulties, it was only after four years that the Empire was reported as making 'rapid strides towards financial improvement'.[25] Finally, it was thought in 1902

'not beyond the utter bounds of possibility that at the next half-yearly meeting of the Empire Variety Theatre in Victoria Square a dividend may be declared. Certainly, it will be near time, considering that the pretty resort will soon have reached its seventh year of existence. Though to be sure, it had a somewhat chequered career during at least the earlier half of this period...'[26]

Despite continued occasional grumbling regarding the quality of the pro- grammes provided, the Empire stubbornly carried on its music-hall pro- grammes, even when others began to fall away. It 'struggled on'[27] through the advent of silent-picture houses, and in a curious twist, combated the arrival of the 'talkies' in the 1930s in part with serious drama. In 1929 began the era of The Empire Players (the Belfast Repertory Theatre Company), a resident company at the theatre. Founded by Richard Hayward and J.R. Mageean, who had recently left the Ulster Theatre, its shows proved enormously pop- ular and a succession of highly successful productions were staged, most notably original works by Thomas Carnduff. Hayward stated that 'The idea was... that we should show the public that we could give them plays, carefully produced'.[28] The company featured a roll-call of some of the finest actors in the Ulster theatre at this time, including R.H. MacCandless, Dan Fitzpatrick, Nan Cullen, Mimi Mageean, Elizabeth Begley and Jack Gavin. Mageean pro- duced and acted in most of the plays staged by the company, earning a sheaf of excellent reviews which are neatly summarised by a 1933 *Irish Times* refer- ence to 'almost unbelievably fine acting.'[29] Ideally, Hayward thought a per- manent home would be found for the company. In the meantime, however, the company had a good working relationship with the Empire and its man- ager, Gerald Morrisson; the latter adjusted theatre policy to suit the company on occasion, and cancelled, for example, the Empire's long-standing policy of twice-nightly shows for *Machinery* by Carnduff 'to enable the cast to do full justice to the theme.'[30]

In the sense that the company presented a set of working-class dramas about urban Belfast to a working-class Empire audience, the Belfast Repertory Company's plays were unique events. The company's activities were fully supported; well-filled houses were 'usually the case for a Belfast Repertory Theatre production'.[31] However, varying accounts exist of the theatre's atmosphere on these occasions. *Workers*, Carnduff's drama of the shipyards utilising working class speech 'for the first time in Ulster drama'[32] was presented in lieu of the usual variety fare in 1932. The audience was reported in the *Irish News* as having

> 'not only applauded warmly at the final curtain, but also throughout the action of the play, many of the forceful lines exciting spontaneous approval.'[33]

Conversely, the *Northern Whig* noted

> 'The Belfast working man who pays his weekly 6d or 1s for a night's entertainment, with all respects to his other admirable qualities, is not the dog on which to try a new play, even one that delineates a side of his own... Perhaps tragedy lies too near his own door for him to accept more when it comes by way of the theatre. Whatever the reason, he and his womenfolk came near to ruining Carnduff's play. The dramatic force of the first act, which sometimes reached fine heights, was time and again shattered by bursts of laughter, though what humour there is in the bitter antagonism of two men itching to be at each other's throats is beyond ordinary comprehension... Full as the house was, it would have been better half-filled than to have had those awful gusts of laughter.'[34]

Nonetheless, the company carried on to stage *Machinery* (1933), *Traitors* (1934) and *Castlereagh* (1934) by Carnduff at the Empire and Abbey Theatres. It also presented stage versions at the theatre of the Ulster comedy films in which the players featured, *Luck of the Irish* and *The Early Bird*. Overall, the company was declared 'a power in the land', with Hayward 'unswerving from his purpose of creating something which will be as vital a force in the dramatic life of Northern Ireland as is the Abbey Theatre in the South.'[35] However, despite its considerable success and Hayward's hopes that the company could eventually 'establish a permanent Repertory Theatre in Belfast',[36] this was not to happen. Bell says the company folded shortly after its production in December 1937 of two one-act plays by Hugh Quinn at the Gaiety Theatre, *Collecting the Rent*, and *A Quiet Twelfth*. Of its work, the *Belfast Telegraph* stated that 'Mr. Gerald Morrison and the directors of the Empire Theatre have earned the gratitude of the general public for their support in the development of the dramatic life of Ulster...'[37]

After the Belfast Repertory Company experiment, the Empire Theatre reverted to its main business of variety for a number of years. Subsequently, business was badly hit by the next major development in popular entertainment, television. Mr. G.D. Findlater (the theatre had remained a family concern) stated that 'TV competition in the variety field is too strong for a local theatre',[38]and rumours began to circulate in the late 1950s that the theatre would close. In 1960 the theatre received a reprieve with the presentation of *Over the Bridge*, Sam Thompson's play which was controversially taken out of production by the Ulster Group Theatre in 1959. Instead, it premiered at the Empire Theatre on January 26, 1960 at the invitation of the then manager, Frank Reynolds. Produced by James Ellis, who had resigned from the board of the Ulster Group Theatre in protest at its *Over the Bridge* decision, the play was staged by Ulster Bridge Productions, a new company formed by Ellis, Henry Lynch Robinson and Thompson. It became a huge success. During a six week run at the theatre, it was seen by over 42,000 people, an unprecedented audience for a play in Belfast. It then went on tour to Dublin, Glasgow, Brighton and London.

During the Ulster Bridge Productions tour, G.D. Findlater announced changes to the Empire Theatre company's articles of association. Mr. James Ellis was to be co-opted onto the Board, and the number of directors increased from two to seven with the long term aim of making the Empire into the 'National Theatre' of the North. The theatre would, stated Findlater, present more new plays by local authors staged by local producers. It would also encourage local operatic and dramatic societies to make frequent use of the theatre.[39] This decision was prompted in part by the success of *Over the Bridge*, but also by the fact that cross-channel companies of merit were now choosing more lucrative television performances rather than the stage as their first priority. Few Irish companies existed north or south that could attract big enough audiences to make the shows paying propositions.

Unfortunately, though a few productions were staged, Findlater's plans for a 'National Theatre' were short-lived and the Empire Theatre was bought soon afterwards by Littlewoods. The theatre was closed on June 3, 1961. A campaign headed by David Luke, the former PR consultant to the theatre, ensued to keep the theatre open at least until its demolition date, but without success. The Empire Theatre was finally demolished in early October 1962. The roll-call of those who had performed on its stage included Charlie Chaplin, Marie Lloyd, Vesta Tilley and George Formby. Commentators declared that the Empire Theatre was ultimately characterised throughout its history by 'an awareness of public taste and a willingness to meet it'.[40] This affectionately remembered theatre lasted longer as a venue solely and continuously dedicated to live performance than any other erected during the music-hall years.

Grand Opera House, Belfast (1895–)

Despite a chequered history, the Grand Opera House, Belfast has 'become one of the city's best-loved landmarks'[41] since its opening by J.F. Warden on December 16, 1895. The theatre's origins have been detailed in the previous chapter, and a full history of the theatre, *The Grand Opera House, Belfast* by Lyn Gallagher, was published in 1995 to mark its centenary year. A good overview is also provided in the 1980 publication, *Frank Matcham, Theatre Architect,* edited by Brian Mercer Walker. However, salient features in all such accounts include the following:

For some time after an initially good opening period, the Grand Opera House endured difficulties in attracting audiences to performances of serious theatre. Hence, in 1904 the theatre changed its orientation and title from the Grand Opera House and Cirque to the Palace of Varieties. This new designation lasted five years, during which time the theatre presented variety shows, with legitimate drama being staged at the Theatre Royal. In 1909, the theatre reverted to its original name and purpose as a venue for mixed programmes featuring opera, ballet, drama and pantomime. During World War II, this was necessarily adjusted due to travel restrictions, and a resident repertory company called the Savoy Players was introduced by the then manager Edward Buckley. The Players performed contemporary plays twice-nightly during the war years; after the war ended, the touring companies returned. However, in 1949 George Lodge, General Manager of the Imperial Cinema and Cinematograph theatres, bought a controlling interest in the Grand Opera House. Though 'the theatre continued in its traditional role'[42], Lodge also began to introduce cinema programmes, and in 1960 sold the Grand Opera House to the Rank Odeon group. Rank made some physical alterations to the theatre, but promised to continue the policy of mixing live shows and films.[43] As a cinema the Opera House was, however, 'something of a disaster'[44]; combined with the increasing popularity of television, and the advent of the Ulster troubles, it soon began to represent a poor investment. Hence, in 1972 Rank Odeon closed the Opera House and soon afterwards, the theatre was sold to a firm of property developers. Two years later, 'with demolition imminent'[45], it became the beneficiary of intense lobbying by the Ulster Architectural Heritage Society for the statutory listing of Northern Ireland buildings of architectural merit. In 1974 the Grand Opera House became the first building in Belfast to be so listed and, in 1976, the theatre was purchased by the Arts Council of Northern Ireland. Given the circumstances both inside and outside the building at the time, this act 'took a considerable and highly imaginative act of faith'.[46] Major restoration work began under the guidance of Robert McKinstry, and took almost four years to complete. The programme of conservation and rehabilitation had a cost 'approaching £3 million', which was met by instalments from the Department of Education.[47] When the Grand Opera House re-opened on September 15, 1980, it was hailed as 'an aesthetically satisfying and technically efficient theatre'[48] and under the management of Michael Barnes became once again a home for opera, ballet, pantomime and popular and serious drama. It was badly damaged by a 1000lb bomb in December 1991, but re-opened within nine months. In May 1993 the theatre suffered a second bomb attack, and was more extensively damaged. However, it 'was able to mount a pantomime seven months later'.[49] In April 1994 the Grand Opera House was leased to a board of trustees by the Arts Council, which had decided that the theatre would operate more effectively if independently controlled. Since then, under the directorship of Derek Nicholls, the Grand Opera House has remained 'a vital part of Belfast life'.[50] Over the years it has hosted stars from Sarah Barnhardt to Orson Welles, and organisations from the Frank Benson Company to Kenneth Branagh's Renaissance Company. There has also been a long-standing and fruitful relationship between the Grand Opera House and the amateur drama movement in Northern Ireland.

Royal Hippodrome (1907–1997), Belfast

The Royal Hippodrome was built at Glengall Place on the site of a former terrace of four five-storey buildings.[51] The theatre was opened on Easter Monday, April 1, 1907 by the Belfast Hippodrome Company Limited late into the variety and music hall boom. No expense was spared on the theatre; designed to seat 2,200, the *Belfast News-Letter* effusively described it as

> 'the handsomest place of entertainment in Ireland... Entering by either of the principal doors from Great Victoria Street – one leading to the stalls and private boxes, the other to the circle – the visitor is at once impressed with the fact that neither money nor pains have been spared... The roof is hand-painted in a delicate and charming design of roses and flowers, the wall decorations are simple and chaste and a rich velvety carpet in harmony with its surroundings completes the design... On the stage the scenery is painted in bright and pleasing, but never garish colours, and many of the scenes are exceedingly fine... [a] novel feature – at least so far as local places of amusement are concerned – is the ingenious system by which the footlights are concealed from the view of the audience, being placed on a continuous shield, thus throwing all the light on to the stage.'[52]

The first bill gives a good indication of the nature of Royal Hippodrome presentations. The two performances at 6.50 and 9 p.m. featured a baby impersonator, a comedian and dancer, the Martelloni troupe of lady acrobats, McCann's Irish Terriers, comedian Horace Wheatley, Hipposcope pictures and a magic album of picture postcards. However, The Hippodrome was also one of the earliest theatres to include film in its design.[53] One of the items accorded much attention at its opening was

> 'the structure containing the cinematograph apparatus. Nowadays no entertainment is considered complete without a medley of moving films giving a vivid impression of striking scenes in all parts of the world... the lantern is a magnificent one, throwing a strong and steady light... with its fireproof walls and asbestos emergency shutters, it not only ensures safety inside the house, but keeps out all unpleasant fumes...'[54]

The theatre was therefore equipped to show films together with variety acts throughout the silent era.[55] By 1925, however, there were 11 silent-picture houses in west Belfast alone,[56] and by the 1930s competition increased further with the introduction of the 'talkies'. Hence, in 1931 it was announced by Associated British Cinemas Ltd. that the Hippodrome was to cease business as a variety theatre; the orchestra, stage hands and attendants were given notice to leave in June of that year. On July 20, 1931 the theatre re-opened as a 'talkie' cinema. Crowds queued patiently outside to gain admittance to *Resurrection* and *Bad Sister*, its first showing.[57] In 1939, however, a live pantomime, *Cinderella*, ran at the theatre and was a success. As a result, Mr. David Forester, the then manager, decided to 'recapture for the Hippodrome its old music-hall glory by bringing to it some of the finest revues and variety programmes that are touring Britain today'.[58] In May 1942 this was taken a step further when the Hippodrome introduced a resident band for this 'cine-variety',[59] which mixed film and live shows in the one programme.

In 1961 Odeon (Northern Ireland) Ltd. became the new proprietors of the Hippodrome, and announced that the building was to become their flagship theatre in Northern Ireland.[60] Now called the Odeon, the theatre was closed for extensive improvements and renovations; in September it was stated that the outside was getting 'a thorough face-lift' while the inside was being ripped out.[61] On October 14, 1961 it re-opened with *Come September* and *The Guns of Navarone*. Commentators noted that

> 'the lavish gilt and plush boxes are hidden now and the steeply raked gallery − known fondly as the 'Gods' − has disappeared behind the strangely angled roof. The overwhelming grandeur, so much a part of the old theatre, has been submerged in the clean sweeping lines of modern comfort. The massive 2,200-seater theatre, so impressive in its size and eccentricity of form and furnishing, ultra-modern in its own day, has given place to a cinema seating 1500... All external trace of the old Hippodrome is to go...'[62]

In the early 1970s incendiary devices were periodically left at the Odeon Cinema, as well as others. In 1974 the Rank organisation announced that it was pulling out of Northern Ireland, and its 14 cinemas, owned by a subsidiary company Rank Odeon (Northern Ireland) were to be bought by a consortium of Northern Ireland businessmen. On completion of the sale, the theatre was re-named the New Vic, and used mainly for cinema presentations, though occasional shows also took place there. Michael Open, in his book *Fading Lights, Silver Screens*, described

> 'a certain sadness about the place for, as the last big cinema auditorium in Belfast, its cinema presentations are virtually never full... [it] gives the impression of being a cinematographic anachronism lost between a glorious past and an uncertain future.'[63]

Architecturally, too, after its renovations over the years the edifice was deemed:

> 'an entirely uninteresting building with bright plastic portico, corrugated metal cladding and flat roof, inside which the eyes go down four times daily for Bingo sessions... However, the present facade is said to

have been attached to Bertie Crewe's building... it would be intriguing to see the old structure exposed and restored at some future date.'[64]

Such speculation ended in November 1996, when the Hippodrome was demolished to make way for an office block.

The Twentieth Century

'Take care, Owen. To remember everything is a form of madness.'
— *Translations* by Brian Friel.

The Ulster Literary Theatre (1902–1934)

This Ulster has its own way of things...[1]
We have not striven to erect a barrier between Ulster and the rest of
Ireland; but we aim at building a citadel in Ulster for Irish thought and
art achievements such as exists in Dublin. If the result is provincial rather
than national it will not be our fault, but due to local influences over
which we have no control, but which we shall not deliberately nourish
and cultivate...[2]

Uladh, the Literary and Critical Magazine of the Ulster Literary Theatre

Relative to the dearth of material available on other theatre companies
in Ulster, the Ulster Literary Theatre has been awarded reasonably
comprehensive critical attention. This includes two chapters in Sam
Hanna Bell's *The Theatre in Ulster*[3], Rutherford Mayne's 1955 piece, *The Ulster
Literary Theatre*[4], and almost the entire first section of Hagal Mengel's *Sam
Thompson and Modern Drama in Ulster*.[5] Anecdotal information is given in
Whitford Kane's *Are We All Met?*, while Dr. Margaret McHenry's 1931 D.Phil.
thesis for the University of Pennsylvania, *The Ulster Theatre in Ireland*, provides
substantial historical detail. It features a a year-by-year account of the company's history, together with a chronological list of first productions, and a
short evaluation of its work. Augmenting these sources is the Ulster Literary
Theatre's own literary and critical magazine, *Uladh*, of which four editions
were produced between 1904 and 1905. The range of topics *Uladh* covered is
'incredibly wide, and there is not a single article in all four issues which does
not somehow respond to the specific tensions within the province.'[6] Given
such coverage, only the cardinal facts of the company's history are herein
described.

Founded in 1902 by two members of the Protestant National Association,
Bulmer Hobson and David Parkhill (Lewis Purcell), the Ulster Literary
Theatre aimed to "use the Drama for propoganda purposes", hoping to
'spread the ideas and principles of Wolfe Tone and the United Irishmen'.[7]
The company initially designated itself the Ulster branch of the Irish National
Literary Theatre, and planned to stage Yeats' *Cathleen Ni Houlihan* as one of
their first productions. Expecting to gain the support of the National Theatre
Society in Dublin in this, they contacted the group and found found most of
their Dublin counterparts "most cordial and helpful".[8] Yeats, however, alone
proved 'haughty and aloof',[9] and correspondance was eventually sent by
George Roberts, the Dublin secretary, to Parkhill

'informing him that the Belfast actors had no authority to state that they
were a branch of the Irish National Literary Theatre. At the same time,
he demanded royalties from the impoverished company... The
Ulstermen's answer was simple and direct. They renamed their company
the Ulster Literary Theatre and applied themselves to the writing of
their own plays.'[10]

Though *Cathleen Ni Houlihan* eventually did become, jointly with James Cousins' *The Racing Lug*, the first production of the new company in 1902, the focus of the company by 1904 had therefore changed to original work by Ulster writers. The first two plays produced in that year under the company's new title, *The Reformers* by Purcell and *Brian of Banba* by Bulmer Hobson, were quite successful, the former being written specifically for the ULT and the latter having recently been published in *The United Irishman*. They were staged in the context of the declarations of *Uladh*, the company's literary magazine, the first edition of which had appeared in November 1904. This contended that

'Uladh means Ulster. It is still often necesary to state as much, we intend to insist... This Ulster has its own way of things, which may be taken as the great contrast to the Munster way of things, still keeping on Irish lands... We intend to strike our keynote through the Theatre where our own plays will be produced, and to let that discover our pathway for us and voice these aims and hopes and hatreds and loves best expressed that way... We recognise at the outset that our art of the drama will be different from that other Irish art of drama which speaks from the stage of the Irish National Theatre in Dublin... At present we can only say that our talent is more satiric than poetic. That will probably remain the broad difference between the Ulster and the Leinster schools... There is a strong undercurrent of culture in the North, and this we will endeavor to tap, and, if possible, turn into native channels... We may roll the stone that has been only pushed at by others. Then will the heroes of the North ride forth again, at present they only sleep within the cavern of dark prejudice and ignorance and distrust.'[11]

Even within the group, this statement aroused controversy. Until the magazine's demise, *Uladh* contributors debated whether the ULT was raising consciousness of the intrinsic values of the province, 'still keeping on Irish land', or actually seeking a form of secessionism. In the meantime, the productions of the new theatre continued apace. The first two plays staged by the ULT had featured actors Dudley Digges and Maire Quin from Dublin; from 1904 onwards they were peopled by their own members, including newcomers from the School of Art Sketching Club which had folded in 1904. These were 'greatly to enrich its fortunes and future',[12] featuring, amongst others, the Morrow brothers, Jack, Edwin, Fred and Harry, W. R. Gordon, James Hodgen and John McBurney. Of the acting, it was said in *Uladh* in February 1905 that

'as yet it has not the spontaneity or the ripeness that distinguishes the Dublin Theatre, but the performances... proved once and for all that there is no real ground for the fears expressed by Uilliam Donn in the first number of this magazine, that the Ulster temperament would prove an insuperable bar to success on the stage. The ease and dignity with which the players performed their parts came as a pleasant surprise...

There was little or no self-consciousness, and all worked together for the success of the pieces in a way that is very rare in amateur companies.'

The final edition of Uladh declared that 'the acting of the ULT continues to improve with each performance', and indeed, Bell states that over its subsequent thirty year history, 'almost every Ulster actor of note appeared at some time in the Theatre's productions'.[13]

The plays in which these actors appeared were written in the main by members of the Theatre. As the group developed, the nationalist component of the plays disappeared very rapidly, and the emphasis fell upon the 'social reality of the Province, including its historical developments and traditions'.[14] The plays which resulted were, it has been suggested, 'on a domestic scale, with none of Yeats' vistas of a poetic barony'.[15] Mengel states, however, that

> 'The experimental phase, during which the ULT had been able to find its particular artistic and political line according to the standards set by Uladh, lasted even less than ten years. Of the plays which were written during this period some merit special attention, as they had a highly formative influence on the entire theatre movement in Ulster, forming the mould of something which might be called 'the Ulster play'.[16]

Mengel includes among these influential works Lewis Purcell's *The Enthusiast*, Rutherford Mayne's *The Turn of the Road* (1906) and *The Drone* (1908), and Gerald MacNamara's *Suzanne and the Sovereigns* (1907) and *Thompson in Tir-na-nOg* (1912). If these frequently 'bore an impression of experimental incompleteness',[17] they nonetheless

> 'for the first time, put ordinary Ulster people in everyday Ulster dress, speaking contemporary Ulster dialect, before theatre audiences throughout these islands.'[18]

With at least one new play being produced each season, the ULT repertoire grew over the years until, by 1934, it had premiered some forty-seven one-act and full-length works both written and produced by the company.[19] Though these included comedies, tragedies, farce, melodrama, and problem plays, satire predominated in the ULT programme. This could be quite daring, with the plays of MacNamara (a pseudonym for Harry C. Morrow), in particular, being

> 'absolutely topical, full of innuendo not just about the contemporary political and social scene, but also its historical background. When his first play *Suzanne* was first produced in 1907, everybody expected a terrible uproar from enraged loyalists. Likewise, MacNamara's classic *Thompson in Tir-na-nOg* was held to be safe fare only under the protective wing of the tried success *The Drone* by Rutherford Mayne. There were no disturbances at any of these occasions...'[20]

Such work made MacNamara one of the most important dramatists of the ULT, and his eight plays proved stalwart favourites with local audiences. So, too, did the works of Rutherford Mayne. Described in *The Irish Theatre* as the most impressive playwright of the Ulster Literary Theatre, Mayne contributed nine plays in total to the ULT. These included only one realistic comedy, *The Drone*, which became the piece-de-resistance of the ULT. Of his other plays, such as the tragedies *Red Turf* (1911) and *The Captain of the Hosts* (1910), or the farce *If* (1914), it has been said that a

> 'muffled lyricism and a sympathy for the characters not always evident in the Cork realists or St. John Ervine gain for them a measure of distinctiveness.'[21]

Together with Mayne and MacNamara, names such as Lynn Doyle, Charles K. Ayre, and Robert Christie also featured on the playwright's list of the company. The writer George Shiels had his first two plays, *Under the Moss* and *Felix Reid and Bob* produced by the ULT under the pseudonym George Morshiel in 1918 and 1919 respectively.

By the late teens of the new century, however, the ULT's initial driving force and enthusiasm was waning. It had already achieved a great deal. Forrest Reid thought that the period up to 1912 was the Theatre's 'happiest period'.[22] During this time, the theatre regularly, and successfully, toured to Dublin, with initial seasons at the Abbey Theatre in March 1907, April 1908 and November 1909. Of the first tour, Joseph Holloway wrote: 'What the company lacks is finish; the players have talent and plenty to spare'.[23] Yeats recalled of the plays:

> 'the absence of the ordinary conventions, the novelty of movement and intonation... It was in their mechanism that their playwrights failed. It was in their delight in the details of life that they interested one... the Ulster Players are the only dramatic society, apart from our own, which is doing serious artistic work.'[24]

After 1910, the ULT tended to stage their Dublin seasons at the Gaiety Theatre. In that same year, indicating the increasing popularity of the Theatre, it also moved its Belfast production venue. Having staged its initial productions at the smaller Ulster Minor Hall in 1904 and 1906, at Clarence Place Hall in 1905 and at the Exhibition Hall from 1907 to 1909, the Grand Opera House thereafter became the home of its work. London and American tours were also undertaken. In May 1911 the company travelled under the management of Whitford Kane to Kelly's Theatre, Liverpool and to the Gaiety, Manchester. In February 1912 the ULT performed a series of matinees, again under Kane's management, at the Royalty Theatre, London. This resulted in a tour to the United States in December 1912, with performances at Washington, Baltimore and New York of Mayne's *The Drone*. The play closed at the latter venue after only two performances, with Kane accusing the American manager, William A. Brady, of having adjusted the script for the worse in giving it a stage-Irish nature. Nevertheless, on the company's return, the ULT continued to have 'years of fruition',[25] and consolidated its position over the next number of years as a regular producer of new work. Bell states that this middle period ended in approximately 1920, but Forrest Reid notes that 'in 1916 that split in the camp which seems to be inevitable in the growth of all such enterprises occurred, and several of the leading actors... resigned.'[26]

No explanation for this split is provided. All agree, however, that in Gerard Morrow's words:

'the ten years from 1924 to 1934 were the most difficult of the Theatre's existence, and also the most uninteresting. Although fifteen new productions took place in the ten years there was none of outstanding merit and few, if any, could be revived at the Opera House.'[27]

This has been variously explained; Bell mentions 'the frenetic politics of the period' and the fact that many of the old ULT members had emigrated.[28] Mengel notes the 'almost clannish group consciousness which developed within the ULT...The result was bound to be stagnation first, then decline in the quality of the programme...'[29] Whitford Kane thought the theatre needed a subsidy to survive.[30] In 1930, two ULT players, Richard Hayward and J.R. Mageean, made a take-over bid for the leadership of the Ulster Theatre (the word 'Literary' had been dropped in February 1915), seeking to put it 'on a more commercial and professional footing'.[31] Failing in their attempt, they left the Theatre, and founded instead the Belfast Repertory Company, which assumed the mantle of staging new writing for a period. 1934 was the Ulster Theatre's last year at the Opera House. Having lost money in that season, the company was thereafter 'refused the stage they had filled with such distinction for twenty-six years'.[32] The Ulster Theatre had, since 1904, developed to a high degree an 'artistic reflection of attitudes, manners, language, environments, and the specific problems pertaining to social life in the province and Belfast.'[33] Its work had 'paved the way for successive generations of Ulster writers'. The ULT actors had 'raised a tradition of living theatre in Ulster'.[34] David Kennedy states that it would be difficult to find in the history of Ulster another movement 'which attracted such a galaxy of talent and in which men and women of such diverse creeds and political views were united in a common purpose.'[35] However, for audience members, such as the thirteen-year-old future writer and journalist Cathal O'Shannon in 1905, the existence of the company simply meant that

'for the first time I saw the kind of people that I knew and lived among in Co. Antrim and Co. Derry were there alive and talking as they talked at home... I was very much impressed.'[36]

The Northern Drama League (1923–1939)

The Northern Drama League was founded in 1923 'to promote amateur performances of such good plays as are unlikely to be produced in the theatres of the city'. The proposing committee of R.V. Williams (Chairman), H.L. Morrow (Hon. Secretary), H. Anderson (Hon. Treasurer), L. Gaffikin, W.R. Gordon, Richmond Noble and Professor H.O. Meredith suggested in an initial circular that that the League would 'aim at simplicity and economy of setting, and the presentation of each play by an intelligent and sympathetic cast…There is no desire that the plays should make a profit'.[37]

The Northern Drama League's first season took place at the Great Hall of Queen's University Belfast, and included a production by Queen's University Dramatic Society. Thereafter, though a link with the University remained, the League performed at the Central Hall, Rosemary Street. A subscription society, its members enrolled in the categories either of 'audience' or 'active participants'. The plays performed by the League lived up to the initial aims propounded by its founders, and the NDL staged, despite 'the limitations of the hall',[38] an impressive range of non-commercial plays over some sixteen years. These included classics by Euripides and Shakespeare; drama by more recent authors such as Chekhov, Ibsen, Synge, Shaw, Marlowe, Gogol, Strindberg, Tolstoi; and (less regularly) plays by local writers such as Richard Rowley, Lynn Doyle and Professor H.O. Meredith. The company also premiered *Blind Man's Buff* in January 1938, a collaborative play by Denis Johnston and Ernst Toller. Reviews invariably mention strong performances, and actors associated with the company included R.H. MacCandless, Jack McQuoid, Cicely Mathews, Nita Hardie and Jean Hamilton.

In 1929 the Northern Drama League initiated the Northern Dramatic Feis. This popular competition for amateur drama groups took place on an annual basis initially at the Empire Theatre, and from 1934 onwards at the Grand Opera House. It featured groups as varied as the Ministry of Labour Dramatic Society, the Belfast Jewish Institute, the Lisburn British Legion Dramatic Society, the Pride of Erin, the Carrickfergus Repertory Players, the Queen's University A.D.S. and the Bangor Unemployed Men. Library records for the Feises end in 1937, and there are no press details of Feises taking place during the spring of 1938 or 1939. The League itself was dissolved in 1939. In his 1951 review of the theatre in Ulster, David Kennedy stated that 'almost every amateur actor in Belfast had some association with the League', aand added that its work deservedly earns it a 'special place' in the history of the amateur movement.[39]

(Full production list in archive catalogue)

The Little Theatre, Belfast (1932–1937)

The Little Theatre, Belfast was founded in 1932, and for four years thereafter presented a range of standard repertory productions weekly at the Ulster Minor Hall. Two of its originators, L. Griffith-Knight and his wife, Doris Richmond, came to Belfast from England on tour in 1932 and decided to operate a small company in Ulster. This had little success, but later that year the couple met Nicholas O'Donnell Grimshaw and the three founded a new venture together, the Belfast Thespians Repertory Company. Two productions followed, *Blackmail* by Charles Bennett and *The Lion and the Mouse* by Charles Klein at the Central Hall, Rosemary Street. Encouraged by this experiment, the company rented the Ulster Minor Hall in January 1933 from the City Council for a season and redecorated it, installing a stage and some lighting.[40] Now re-named the Little Theatre Repertory Company, they opened there on January 30, 1933 with *The Yellow Ticket* by Michael Morton. An announcement followed that the company intended to put on a new play every week, with 'popular prices the rule'. It also stated that

> 'one or two professionals assist the players already mentioned [Knight and Richmond] and the various roles in the different plays are filled by well-known amateurs, glad to get stage experience of this kind... They do not intend to produce Ulster dialect plays, feeling that existing Ulster repertory companies and amateur companies are keeping that side of the theatre before the public.'[41]

Attendance at this first production was 'meagre',[42] though the *Belfast Telegraph* reviewer believed the performance was 'of far more than average amateur calibre'. However, a later review noted that 'only for a period of a few weeks at the start before it was known at all, did the company play to poor houses. Very soon the luck turned...'[43] Focusing its presentations primarily on comedies by contemporary playwrights, the Little Theatre temporarily found a niche in the city. Knight believed that

> 'people of a city so largely industrial as Belfast have no flair for tragedy or sombre dramatic fare unless written by a very well-known modern author...Comedies, either modern or costume by modern authors, evoke the best patronage, but present day Belfast, in his experience, does not react at all enthusiastically to Shakespeare or any of the old classics.'[44]

The Little Theatre's programming exemplified these beliefs, with large-scale productions proving a speciality. A number of plays were produced using very large casts – *Children in Uniform* had an all-female cast of 29, *The Rose Without a Thorn* featured 18 people on stage and Cornelius was staged with a cast of 19. No particular emphasis fell on Irish work, dialect or non-dialect. One work by each of St. John Ervine, C.K. Munro, Ruddick Millar, Harry Gibson and Denis Johnston was produced in the four years; the latter granted permission to the Little Theatre to première his *Moon in the Yellow River* in Ireland.

Audiences seem to have been reasonable for the company's productions on occasion. However, in summer 1936 the Little Theatre toured to Bangor, thereby introducing the first real break in the company's Belfast run of productions since its foundation. On its return, the Little Theatre experienced very disappointing attendances. In December the City Council, having already served notice on the company that its contractual obligations were not being fulfilled, gave 'the usual notification to those responsible...'[45] The Little Theatre managed to re-open almost immediately, but declared itself in difficulties. In April 1937 the local press reported that it had 'reluctantly been compelled to close down owing to an extraordinary lack of public support and appreciation of the excellent work it did in the interests of dramatic art in the city.'[46]

The Playhouse, Belfast (1937–1939)

The Playhouse was founded in 1937 when Mr. Harald Norway took over the defunct Little Theatre at the Ulster Minor Hall and decided to run it as a repertory theatre 'on new lines'.[47] It was, he declared, to be a home 'not only for a resident company but also for all the other play-producing bodies in the Province'.[48] This aspiration was reflected in the membership of the Advisory Board, which included many of the most well-known figures in drama in Ulster at the time, such as J.R. Mageean, R.H. MacCandless, Gerald Morrow and David Kennedy. The Playhouse opened at the Ulster Minor Hall on May 3, 1937 with a performance of *Night Must Fall* by Emlyn Williams. Plays produced thereafter changed generally on a week-by-week basis, with Norway as the manager, producer, and often leading actor. Music was provided by the 'Playhouse Trio', and tickets cost from 6d for the pit to 2/4 for the orchestra stalls. A Playhouse Circle was founded, with talks and recitations, and a 'Playhouse School of Elocution and Dramatic Art', run by Miss Jean Hamilton, was also initiated. Requests for 'Ulster plays, Ulster playwrights, Ulster players' appeared regularly in the Playhouse programmes. Despite this, the emphasis of the Playhouse in practice did not fall on Ulster writing particularly. Of a list of plays proposed by the Advisory Board in May 1937, which favoured such writers as Peadar O'Donnell, Yeats, Mayne and Carnduff, few were actually produced, and by March 1938 the names of the Advisory Committee no longer appear in the programmes. Nevertheless, the theatre carried on producing plays by writers such as Noel Coward, A.W. Pinero, George Bernard Shaw, Ivor Novello and R.C. Sherriff until 1939, when, on February 13, it was reported that sheriff's officers

> 'seized scenery and other property owned by Mr. Harald Norway, the actor-manager. In the Northern Ireland High Court on Thursday the Lord Chief Justice granted an order for final judgement in an action brought by Belfast Corporation against Mr. Norway to recover £42 11s 11d balance due for arrears of rent of the Ulster Minor Hall up to February 16.'[49]

The Playhouse Theatre did not re-open following this financial crisis. However, the years of the Little Theatre and Playhouse experiments firmly established the Ulster Minor Hall as a centre for regular theatre-going – an important fact which was noted with interest by the flourishing local amateur drama movement. Under its auspices, the short seven-year history of the theatre at the Ulster Minor Hall would shortly become the groundwork for a new theatre project of considerable import.
(Full production list in archive catalogue)

The Ulster Group Theatre

Three distinct eras are discernible in the history of the Group Theatre: the 'old' Ulster Group Theatre (1940–1959), the James Young era (1960–1971), and the current Group Theatre (1976–).

The Ulster Group Theatre (1940–1959)

The Ulster Group Theatre was founded during the war years, a time of considerable amateur drama activity in Ulster. Three amateur groups, the Northern Irish Players, the Ulster Theatre and the Jewish Institute Dramatic Society, decided in 1940 to rent the Ulster Minor Hall to stage a season of plays. Having experienced losses with the Playhouse company, the Estates Committee of the Belfast Corporation demanded £6 a week rent with three months' rent in advance. This was agreed, and a 12 week season began in which each group took the theatre in turn, a week at a time, and retained its separate identity. The title selected for the overall experiment, reflecting its composite nature, was the Ulster Group Theatre. A profit of between £30 and £40 was made on this initial season and the Ulster Group Theatre proper began the following September as an amalgamated company with a single identity. The Ulster Theatre alone 'withdrew from this allegiance'.[50]

The sheer difficulty of what was being attempted is hinted at by the Shiels' correspondence in the archive regarding the Group. As companies such as the Playhouse had failed in their stated aims to concentrate on new Ulster writing, the Group appears, initially at least, to have had to make a concerted effort to overcome a sense of scepticism regarding the new project. Hence, when actor-director R.H. MacCandless attempted to persuade the playwright to provide a play for the company, Shiels says he 'discouraged him all I could' and added that he

> 'took little or no interest in this sort of thing…The pity of it is that I have always seen very vividly what an Ulster Theatre might be, and on various occasions my hope revived, only to be quenched again by some idiot, or set of idiots, talking in terms of 'Charlie's Aunt'. Instead of making Ulster drama the foundation of a Little Theatre, they make it a sort of stop-gap between third-rate English plays.'[51]

The efforts of the company appear to have worked, however, and by February 1941, Shiels was grudgingly changing his mind. After the company's production of *The Jailbird* he admitted 'the Group seems to have done very well.'[52] Likewise, when the company premiered *Borderwine* in 1946, he commented to Kennedy before the latter discussed the play on radio:

> 'There are always weak spots; the Abbey casts were always full of them, with bad interpretation to match. In the latter I should imagine the Group people are pretty sound… Give the directors and actors the lion's share of the praise. And above all, drive home the point that plays which deal with contemporary life in this region are the only sure foundations on which to build an Ulster Theatre.'[53]

Though certainly not always so positive, Shiels' own increasing confidence in the company was evidently shared by others. Over the next twenty years the UGT premiered a significant amount of new work by Ulster writers; this was combined with a programme of classic and international drama, all of which is fully detailed in the production list in the theatre archive catalogue. Together with Shiels, local writers St. John Ervine and Joseph Tomelty featured particularly strongly, and there were premieres of works such as Louis MacNeice's *Traitors in Our Way*, and Brian Friel's play (reportedly his first[54]), *The Doubtful Paradise*. Links were also maintained with the amateur drama companies through an annual drama festival, with new players sometimes being recruited from the performers. Over the years, the company itself became a tight-knit one with a strong reputation for ensemble playing. A number of performers appeared regularly, including actors such as Margaret D'Arcy, John Moss, Jack O'Malley, Dan Fitzpatrick, J.R. Mageean, Doreen Hepburn, James Ellis, Colin Blakeley, John F. Tyrone, Cicely Mathews, Jean Lundy, Barbara Adair, Patrick Magee, Elizabeth Begley, Harold Goldblatt, Patrick McAlinney, Stephen Boyd, Allan McClelland, Denys Hawthorne, Bee Duffell, Catherine Gibson, J.G. Devlin, Joseph Tomelty, and R.H. MacCandless. Combating the often difficult surroundings of the Ulster Minor Hall, with noise from rallies, concerts and boxing matches, they attracted large and loyal audiences during the hey-day of the company. In 1951 many of the Group performers were selected by Tyrone Guthrie to perform in the Northern Ireland Festival Company productions of George Shiels' *The Passing Day, Danger, Men Working* by John D. Stewart and Jack Loudan's adaptation of Shadwell's *The Sham Prince* at the Festival of Britain. The company also toured successfully to England and Scotland, and received invitations to the Moscow Arts Theatre and to the United States.

The 'Over the Bridge' Controversy

By the late 1950s, however, the UGT was in difficulties. In part, the company blamed television for low audiences; in part, there were practical difficulties caused by the Group's own success. Performers, having toured abroad with the company, were being offered contracts by other theatres and in other mediums; keeping a regular company together was beginning to prove increasingly difficult. During this 'lean' period a number of actors and actresses were taken off the permanent staff and wages were reduced.[55] Attempting to confront its problems, the company underwent structural changes. In January 1958 it was announced that the Group was to become a non-profit making trust, with four new directors appointed to the board: Harry McMullan (BBC Head of Programmes), Ritchie McKee, James Ellis and Maurice O'Callaghan.[56] The Memorandum of Association, dated 23 May, 1958, had as its third item that

> 'The Company is established to promote, maintain, improve and advance education, particularly by the production of operas, educational plays and the encouragement of the Arts, including the arts of drama, mime, dancing, singing and music, and to formulate, prepare and establish schemes therefor provided that all objects of the Company shall be of a charitable nature.'

The subscribers to the Memorandum and the Articles of Association were James Ellis, Daniel Fitzpatrick, Harold Goldblatt, John James Moss (Solicitor), R.H. MacCandless, John Ritchie McKee, Henry W. McMullan, Maurice O'Callaghan and John J. O'Malley.[57] Having so constituted itself, the Group was awarded a guarantee against loss by CEMA (the Council for the Encouragement of Music and the Arts) for up to £3000.[58] Though this new structure made the financial situation less precarious, both J.G. Devlin and Margaret D'Arcy, very well-known members of the acting company, resigned in December because of dissatisfaction over theatre policy.[59] Harold Goldblatt also resigned as administrator and director of productions, although he remained a director of the company.[60] James Ellis, an acting member, was appointed director of productions in his stead. The company, therefore, was already extremely unsettled going into 1959 when it would face its greatest challenge: the controversy over local shipyard playwright Sam Thompson's work, *Over the Bridge*.

Despite having accepted, cast and held a press-launch for *Over the Bridge* in 1959, the Group directors suddenly decided by a majority of six votes to two to withdraw the play just two weeks before its scheduled production in May.[61] The play had been accepted for production by James Ellis, who had a free hand at selecting and rehearsing plays, as was traditional for the director of productions. According to Hagal Mengel in *Sam Thompson and Modern Drama in Ulster*, Mr. John Ritchie McKee, the Group chairman, saw the script and demanded cuts, which Thompson refused to make.[62] Following the meeting, McKee then famously issued a statement to say that the play was being withdrawn because:

'The Ulster public is fed up with religious and political controversies. This play is full of grossly vicious phrases and situations which would undoubtedly offend and affront every section of the public... It is the policy of the directors of the Ulster Group Theatre to keep political and religious controversies off our stage.'[63]

Thompson was perhaps unfortunate in the timing of this production. It followed a most contentious presentation of *The Bonefire*, written by Gerard McLarnon and directed by Tyrone Guthrie, which had been staged the previous August both at the Grand Opera House and at the Edinburgh Festival. The Belfast production was the subject of considerable media attention, as the play was interpreted in some quarters as an attack on the Orange Order. When it reached Edinburgh, Guthrie was quoted as saying that 'the play had been seen in some quarters as casting a slur on the Orange Order... no such intention was in the mind either of the author or himself.'[64] The play had, it was noted, clearly been re-written in parts for Edinburgh. *The Belfast News-Letter* critic considered that it was now 'now clearly enough a plea for tolerance', but still thought that 'at moments one feels that some Orangemen and women still emerge in a pretty poor light.' Though the reviewer went on to ask 'who is to deny that any large organisation is without its blemished adherents?'[65], nonetheless it was still maintained by some that the Group had stirred up sectarian ill-feeling. This was reinforced by an extract from the Edinburgh programme, which was pointedly quoted in Belfast, questioning whether the North of Ireland might be populous, prosperous, and industrious 'because of, rather than in spite of, the stress of racial, religious and political schism? The stress is there, the strong survive and are strengthened by it; but not all can be strong.'[66]

Hence *The Bonefire* provides the backdrop to the *Over the Bridge* controversy. However, on the first occasion, and despite being a politically 'difficult' drama, the play had been staged. The decision not to do likewise with *Over the Bridge* was deemed inexplicable and indefensible by the majority of the Ulster Group Theatre company. Thompson instituted proceedings against the company for breach of contract, and received a settlement of £175 plus costs.[67] Meanwhile, the company began to collapse. Two of the Group directors, O'Callaghan and Ellis, resigned immediately over the issue. They were closely followed by Harold Goldblatt,[68] and Harry McMullan also resigned citing pressure of work.[69] The acting members were similarly decisive, particularly as a further incident had inflamed the situation. Despite resigning as a company director, James Ellis had continued in the immediate aftermath of the *Over the Bridge* controversy as director of productions with the company. Apparently without informing him, advertisements appeared for an artistic director for the Ulster Group Theatre in July.[70] The English director appointed thereafter, Jonathan Goodman, faced a flood of resignations, and soon no acting member of the company would take part in Group productions. Actress Doreen Hepburn stated:

'The Group Theatre has just disintegrated. I think it ominous that the beginning of the decline can be traced back to the time when non-theatrical directors had more say in the running of the theatre.'[71]

In response Goodman said he was not worried, adding: 'Theatre people are expendable, and when I say that I include myself'.[72] However, Ellis and Thompson were meanwhile busy founding a new company, Ulster Bridge Productions, which staged *Over the Bridge* at the Empire Theatre on January 26, 1960. This proved an enormous success, and featured many of those previously associated with the Group Theatre, including J.G. Devlin, Joseph Tomelty, Irene Bingham, Harold Goldblatt and Ellis himself. Simultaneously, reviews of productions mounted by Goodman at the Group with newcomers were disappointing, and relations between the UGT and local playwrights plummeted. At an informal meeting with some thirty writers, Goodman expressed an interest in continuing to present local work, including plays which 'might risk running into a political storm'. However, he went on to state that

'a regional theatre could not exist on regional plays alone and he intended to present other plays of merit... He expressed the opinion that from an artistic point of view the director of a theatre must be a complete dictator.'[73]

It must also be noted, however, that the writers at this meeting (including Patricia O'Connor, Sam Hanna Bell, John D. Stewart and Jack Loudan) listed a set of grievances built up with the Group Theatre over time: of plays lost, of plays submitted and then returned without comment, of plays accepted and not produced. This bears testimony to the Group's difficulties even before the *Over the Bridge* affair and helps to explain the rapidity with which the company collapsed, if not the events which precipitated that closure.

The James Young Era

Goodman had promised to rectify the practical problems of the Group Theatre; in the event, his opportunity to do so did not arise. Instead, in January 1960, when 'the future looked gloomy indeed',[74] the board of directors announced the acceptance of an invitation which would radically change the nature of the Group: James Young and Jack Hudson had decided to join the theatre to play a season, not as salaried members, but on a percentage basis. Young had formerly appeared with the Group and gone on to make a name for himself in revue as a versatile caricaturist of the Belfast character.[75] He would, he said, 'choose the plays in which I will appear', while Hudson would also 'take charge of the business management at the Group during the season'.[76] By September of that year, Young could announce that the thirteen-week run of the comedy, *The Love Match*, had turned a debit balance into a credit balance at the theatre.[77] Young and Hudson were duly appointed to the board of directors as joint managing directors, with Young producing most of the plays at the Group as well as playing leading parts.[78] When asked for his policy at the theatre, Young said 'It will not be a place of misery and arty-crafty nonsense', and added that he was opposed to the principle of a company of permanent members as 'that could, in my opinion, turn into a repertory company, and actors could be forced to take parts for which they are completely unsuited'.[79] The principle of close ensemble playing, the trademark of the old Ulster Group Theatre, had therefore effectively ended, as had the policy of staging new work by Ulster writers on a regular basis. However, a dozen years of popular success with almost a score of Ulster comedies followed. John Knipe points out that

> 'management was economical and efficient and productions were care-fully planned to meet the taste of the newly emergent audiences; plays were specially commissioned to this end; long runs, laughter and 'House full' notices became the hallmarks of the Group Theatre... the Group ceased to be a suppliant and became a benefactor to other theatres.'[80]

Such beneficiaries included the new Arts Theatre, the Lyric Players Theatre, and the Queen's University Drama Society. In 1961 the Group actually refunded its grant to C.E.M.A. to offset losses in the productions of Brian Friel's *The Doubtful Paradise* and Murphy's *Men on the Wall*. Nevertheless, there was criticism of the new-style Ulster Group Theatre, with Young coming 'under fire for running a slap-happy comedy for 300 performances, to the exclusion of all else on the Group stage.'[81] To these critics came a retort from McKee that 'The 'good old days' consisted of financial failure, with the actors playing very often to audiences of 20.'[82] In June 1964 James Young was elected chairman of the Ulster Group Theatre following the demise of Ritchie McKee, and declared the theatre 'a thriving concern'.[83] During the following years at the theatre Young was to become a much-loved 'genuine original', an 'institution' who, together with his 'faces and cracks, was a first-class character actor'.[84] His era at the Group Theatre was to last until May 1971, when it was announced that the group would close for the summer recess and re-open in mid-August. It did not do so, and the theatre was to remain in darkness during the tensions and social disturbances of the early years of the Troubles.

1976–

In 1976 Belfast City Council, under the guidance of Sir Myles Humphries, decided to re-open the Group Theatre in the hope that it would become the home of amateur drama in Northern Ireland. A new roof, dressing-rooms, lighting, curtains, seating and foyer were installed, and the entire theatre redecorated at a cost of some £80,000.[85] The honour of opening the theatre fell to Bart Players, who staged a special gala performance of *Watch it Sailor* for the first invited audience on November 2, 1973. Actors from the 'old' Group, including Joseph Tomelty, Elizabeth Begley, Stella Davis, Rita Hardie, John F. Tyrone and Charles Witherspoon were present to offer their support.

The re-opening of the Group Theatre, together with the Arts, marked 'the turning of a corner'.[86] The Council's action was to prove, in Bardon's words, 'an inspired decision which was immediately successful'.[87] Just five seasons after opening, the theatre boasted that 41 different amateur drama and operatic companies had presented 121 productions, ranging from the comedies of Sam Cree, pantomimes and high drama, to GCE curriculum plays performed in French, to Shakespeare and George Bernard Shaw. Over 80,000 patrons had already passed through its doors.[88] To this day, the theatre continues the policy proposed in 1976. It provides, appropriately, a central performance venue at a very reasonable charge for the many Ulster amateur drama organisations.

(Full production list for years 1940–1960 has been compiled for the archive catalogue)

The Belfast Arts Theatre

The Belfast Arts Theatre originated as the Mask Theatre, founded by Hubert and Dorothy Wilmot in the 1940s, and located at 33 Linenhall Street, Belfast. There is little record of the work of this early company, save the fact its patrons included 'British and American soldiers who joined the locals to enjoy the plays of Tennessee Williams and Arthur Miller.'[89] In 1946 it was 'compelled to close down owing to the expiration of the lease of the Linenhall Street premises';[90] Bell says their rooms were taken over by the U.S. Army.[91]

However, announcements followed in February 1947 of a new venture, called the Belfast Arts Theatre Studio. This would have its base at 153 Upper North Street and be

> 'an experimental theatre in Belfast, based somewhat on the lines of 'Theatre Workshop' England, but aiming at the development of a definite, individual style.'[92]

For their new endeavour, the Wilmots envisaged a small theatre club. The Arts Theatre Studio was to be a membership theatre seating a maximum of 80 people, with the audience strictly limited to those on the registered list. Wilmot stressed, however, that the theatre was 'by no means an exclusive coterie'; instead, he stated that membership was required because

> '...in these days of prolonged economic difficulty it would be quite impossible to build and equip a theatre, large or small, to fulfil all the conditions laid down by a City Council Licensing Authority. But these regulations do not apply to a membership theatre which is treated as a club open to any member of the public who cares to pay a small annual subscription and register his, or her, name and address...We are a PEO-PLE'S THEATRE.'[93]

The Arts, it was stated, would provide for Belfast 'an international repertory theatre, producing plays of artistic significance hitherto unperformed in Northern Ireland'.[94] Plays were to be selected 'by artistic merit rather than by commercial value'.[95] Initially, times were, Wilmot admitted, 'almost as hard the chairs our unfortunate audience had to sit upon', and audience numbers were low. Slowly, audiences improved until advance booking became necessary, and 'our mailing list was well into three figures'.[96] References were periodically made, however, to difficulties with the 'tiny'[97] North Street venue with its 'stage handicaps – lack of space and equipment',[98] and 'settings achieved under difficult circumstances'.[99] Hence, the Wilmots undertook to find new premises. This was to prove an on-going task. The last performance at the North Street venue, *Our Theatre Scrapbook*, took place in June 1950. In the following October the theatre opened as The Arts Theatre at a larger, 200-seat premises at Fountain Street Mews.[100] Four years later the company moved to Little Donegall Street, where Wilmot had converted 'a disused auction room'[101] to a performance venue seating approximately 200.[102] Again, it proved only adequate for theatre purposes, with Wilmot describing it as being an 'almost insurmountable restricted space'.[103] Finally, on April 17, 1961 the Arts Theatre re-located to its first purpose-built home at Botanic Avenue, where it has remained ever since.

Early reviews lauded the new company, which presented avant-garde programmes featuring writers such as Jean-Paul Sartre, Salacrou, Cocteau and Borchert. The Studio was deemed 'an adventure in playgoing.'[104] Productions generally had short runs, and according to contemporary accounts were well supported. Hubert Wilmot was director-producer, and also contributed a play of his own, *My Name is Wilde*, which was staged in May 1949. Productions by authors such as Pirandello and Anouilh were deemed 'intelligent and challenging'.[105] The success of the theatre can be gauged by the fact that in September 1952 it was announced that performances would take place every night of the week, 'instead of four nights only as formerly, and with a new production every fortnight.'[106] Even with the move to the larger Little Donegall Street premises, the theatre pursued 'a courageous policy of play selection',[107] and continued to alternate plays by writers such as Eliot and Miller every fortnight to three weeks. Its atmosphere was considered in Belfast 'to be 'bohemian' and rather daring.'[108]

1960–1971

The move to Botanic Avenue released Wilmot from the space restrictions at the Arts' previous venues. With a stage 25 feet deep with a 25 feet proscenium opening, and seating for 450,[109] the new theatre marked a vast change in space and ambition from the earlier days of the Arts Theatre Studio. The first play staged there, *Orpheus Descending*, made full use of this new opportunity and featured a cast of 17. A *Belfast Telegraph* leader article proclaimed:

> '...Belfast is extremely fortunate in having a theatre of such high standards... Under Hubert Wilmot's direction, it has brought fine plays to Ulster, and has performed them well. It is now up to the public to give this new venture the added support it deserves... and where it is most needed – at the box office.'[110]

With the increased stage space, however, came box-office concerns for a 450-seat venue. *Belfast Telegraph* reviewer Betty Lowry warned just after the theatre's opening that 'Mr. Wilmot may well begin to think of his future policy and the need to make this as widely-embracing as possible.'[111] Wilmot was conscious of this from the first, and evidently initially believed he could mix his former more esoteric productions with popular fare. A 'fortnightly policy of ringing the changes from gravity to gaiety and back again'[112] was discussed. Even by 1962, however, this policy had begun to disappear. One reviewer asked:

> 'Would you, as a Christie [Agatha] admirer, also go to the Arts for a swing at Inge, a bash at Brecht, a jolt from Bolt, a take-off on Chekhov? I hope you would, but I fear you won't. And 'Hibby' Wilmot seems to have arrived at the same conclusion.'[113]

Wilmot had indeed decided as much. Having discovered his original programming ambitions was not working, he acted swiftly. The local press were told that 'having found thrillers and comedies box-office successes, he has no plans for presenting plays with intellectual appeal'.[114] In the theatre programme, however, Wilmot stated his

> 'regret that I cannot indulge either my own personal taste or that of a sympathetic and quite vocal minority who are not large enough to pay our lighting and heating account for even one week.'[115]

In 1963/4 the Arts Council of Northern Ireland agreed to pay £300 per play for selected works of artistic significance. One of these, *A Midsummer Night's Dream*, was withdrawn due to lack of support, and in July 1964 the Council withdrew from the funding agreement, citing the fact that it was over-expended *Belfast Telegraph*, October 2, 1964. Now a large venue run on a purely commercial basis, light comedies and thrillers began to dominate the Arts programming. A great many productions, one reviewer noted, 'were at best unimaginative. Such plays, as Mr. Wilmot has a little sadly come to recognise, are what the public wants and what will keep the theatre in business.'[116] Neverthetheless, Wilmot's programming attracted full houses until the end of the 1960s, particularly for Ulster writer Sam Cree's comedies which the theatre regularly premiered. The theatre played 'long runs to near-capacity audiences'.[117]

Then came a reported loss of £6,000 in 1969, the first serious deficit the theatre had experienced since its move to Botanic Avenue, and the first public intimation that the future of the theatre had 'been jeopardised by the disturbances'.[118] Wilmot informed the Arts Council of Northern Ireland that as a result of the civil difficulties, the theatre's 'operation was becoming unprofitable.'[119] This prompted much difficulty for the Arts Council. Ordinarily it would hardly consider funding a commercial theatre which had, it stated, 'virtually set aside its interest in drama of any cultural or aesthetic significance'.[120] Should it now do so because of what it termed 'the special circumstances of unrest prevailing in Northern Ireland'?[121] Deliberations on the topic were duly reported in the Annual Reports of the Arts Council for 1969/70, and 1970/71. These noted that the theatre's crisis coincided with a larger debate at the Arts Council regarding the 'perceptible and universal trend towards unprofitibility'[122] of the commercial theatre. In this context, it was stated that the Arts Theatre's profit margins would be expected to decrease in any case, and that the Troubles were

'precipitating the so-called commercial theatre here into the position that other commercial theatres in the United Kingdom are reaching more gradually... The commercial theatre is approaching the threshold of viability that the non-commercial theatre crossed a decade or two ago... This does not necessarily mean that the Arts Council will modify its criteria for subsidy, but it does mean a lot of rethinking will have to be done.'[123]

In short, while the Troubles might appear the problem for the Arts Theatre, the Council believed its underlying difficulty was the unpromising future of the commercial theatre. As a consequence, it was reported that the Arts Council had simply offered to continue its normal subsidies of £500 against loss on each of two Arts Theatre productions for the year 1970/71.[124] Wilmot rejected this as 'totally inadequate'.[125] The Arts Theatre barely struggled on, suffering 'poor audience doldrums' and in January 1971 new pay rates were announced by Equity, the actors' union. Wilmot quoted this as yet another reason why the company would 'close for longer than usual this summer.'[127] The venue was offered to other groups in order to keep the doors open, but by mid-1971 it was proving impossible to do so. The Arts Theatre finally closed on October 14, 1971. Dorothy Wilmot explained that in her opinion, 'If the bombs stopped for two weeks and the buses returned to normal we would open again.'[128] The *Belfast News-Letter* concurred, stating that the theatre had 'fallen a victim to the present unrest in the city, which has deterred many of its patrons from going out in the evenings...'[129] The closure was not to prove permanent, but a phase of the theatre's history had nonetheless ended. Despite Wilmot's best attempts, the Belfast Arts Theatre would not again open as a repertory theatre in the traditional sense of the term.

Interplay

A series of associations with other theatres or theatre forms now began for the Arts Theatre. To meet the immediate difficulty caused by the theatre's closure, the Arts Council decided to create a mobile educational drama unit, Interplay Theatre. This would be based at the Arts Theatre, managed by the Theatre Trust and administered by Hubert Wilmot. Denis Smyth was appointed producer and director. The unit was rapidly established, and a small group of performers such as Stella McCusker and J.J. Murphy began to tour classic and documentary plays to schools audiences throughout Northern Ireland. The imaginative documentary drama programme included *The Titanic, The Age of Change* and *The Batata Blight* by Stewart Love, and *The Trial of Mr. Pickwick* and *The Blue and the Grey*, a play about the American Civil War, by Stewart Parker. The Interplay company was a considerable success. It soon acquired a reputation for excellence, and undertook some regional performances for adults as well as for young people which were very well received. By 1972 it had given 254 performances in 99 schools with 62 schools visiting, and a total of 69,000 young people had seen Interplay in action.[130]

However, on September 15, 1972, and in the midst of Interplay's success, the Arts Theatre building suffered extensive bomb damage, especially to the stage area, making its use for performance purposes impossible. Major repairs and renovations were required. Eventually, it was agreed that these would be largely funded by The Arts Council of Northern Ireland, which would then have access to the theatre for up to 12 weeks of each year for its own promotions.[131] The theatre re-opened on November 11, 1973 for use by Belfast Festival at Queen's, and isolated productions took place there for the next two years. It also continued as a base for Interplay. Then, in mid-1975, the General Purposes and Finance Committee of Belfast City Council agreed in principle to a subsidy for the Belfast Arts Theatre. By November 1976 a package had been put in place. Financial backing for the venture would come both from the Arts Council and the City Council, the latter providing a capital grant of £10,000 as well as a guarantee against loss of up to £20,000 per annum.[132] The Belfast Arts Theatre would re-open on December 16, 1976 with the Ulster Actors' Company's production of *The Mating Season*. Thereafter the UAC would become the resident company at the Arts on a leasing basis.[133] Hubert and Dorothy Wilmot attended the press reception to wish the new company well. They had already moved with Interplay in August 1976 to its new base at the recently completed theatre of the New University of Ulster at Coleraine. In the summer of 1977 Denis Smyth and Hubert Wilmot resigned as Interplay Artistic Director and Administrator respectively, and the company continued until 1980, when it was disbanded, to be 'one of the Province's central theatrical institutions.'[134] Negotiations with Stage 80, which replaced it, coincided with the 'financial contraction'[135] experienced by the Arts Council of Northern Ireland in August 1980, and the following year it was announced that that company too had ceased operations.[136]

The Ulster Actors' Company/Theatre Ulster

Meanwhile, at the Arts Theatre the Ulster Actors' Company took residence to stage 'plays of popular appeal'.[137] Formerly Actors Wild, which had been formed in 1975 by Patrick Galvin, John Anderson, and Roy Heayberd, the company fulfilled its brief, with productions ranging from popular comedies to children's entertainment, variety, and classics. In 1983, the company suffered financial problems; Artistic Director Roy Heayberd and administrator Jim White attributed this to the unpredictable taste of the Ulster theatre-going public.[138] The company postponed its in-house productions from August to December, and offered the theatre for rent to other groups. With this, its residency at the Arts effectively ended.

The theatre itself, however, carried on. In 1984, the newly titled Belfast Civic Arts Theatre entered into a major collaboration, Theatre Ulster. This was a joint management enterprise between the Arts Theatre and the new Riverside Theatre at Coleraine, created to maximise the resources provided by the Arts Council and to ease the financial difficulties faced by both theatres.[139] A small number of productions were staged by Theatre Ulster each year; these included Irish and international classics such as Alan Ayckbourn's *How the Other Half Lives*, Sam Hanna Bell's *That Woman at Rathard*, an adaptation by Sam McCready of Wilde's *The Picture of Dorian Gray*, and Williams' *The Glass Menagerie*. Initially staged at both theatres, the plays then toured to a network of other venues such as the Ardhowen Theatre in Enniskillen. This arrangement continued until 1992, when Theatre Ulster folded.

The Present

Throughout the Theatre Ulster years, the Arts Theatre also continued to host a range of theatrical activities including amateur musicals and performances by local and visiting professional companies. For this it received a general grant from the Arts Council, with major funding being provided by Belfast City Council. This larger funding arrangement continued after the demise of Theatre Ulster, and does so to the present day. The 1986 fund-raising brochure for the theatre declared that the Belfast Civic Arts Theatre 'still holds with a policy of providing people with the best in live entertainment – Drama, Musicals, Dance, Opera and Variety'.[140] Occasional in-house productions are now a feature of Arts Theatre programming, and a Youth Theatre attached to the Arts was founded in 1993. Hence, despite a chequered history and various funding crises, the Arts Theatre has determinedly continued to provide entertainment for the people of Belfast and beyond for almost half a century.

(Full production list for years 1950–1971 in archive catalogue)

The Lyric Players Theatre (1951–)

> This, then, was the reason for beginning: a handful of people interested in the theatre, poetry, and the arts, inspired by a legendary Ulster hero, [who] ignored all obstacles and founded a Poet's Theatre.[141]
>
> — *Mary O'Malley, founder*

From its origins in 1951, the aim of the Lyric Players Theatre was to 'create a style suitable for dramatic poetry'[142] using dance, music and the visual arts. Much of the early impetus was due to the work of Cork woman Mary O'Malley, whose early life was devoted to the theatre and politics. A Labour Councillor for Smithfield, Belfast from 1952–54, O'Malley was also a passionate admirer of the work and principles of W.B. Yeats. In an early lecture, she outlined the founding principles of the company:

> 'When we founded the Lyric Players group in 1951, we had already very definite views on theatre, and we have consistently worked on the basis of these ideals. The restriction to poetic drama was quite deliberate. Interpreted widely, however, it did allow us to include all the world classics (if we so desired) and any good contemporary play could be included on the basis of poetic content in the internal structure... The poetic play also had a special place for the artist and craftsman and permitted experiment in colour, lighting and stagecraft... The total achievement exists only when the theatre is alive with dramatic action and audience response and a harmonious blending of the several arts is present.'[143]

However, O'Malley also added, 'the first thing to be learned in theatre is a form of 'artistic compromise' – making the best of the material at your disposal at all levels'.[144] In this way, the Lyric Players developed a tradition of working in all the art-forms using a combination of pragmatism and quite particular artistic principles. Three phases may be identified in its history: the Derryvolgie years of 1951–mid-1968, when the theatre operated on a private basis from the home of the O'Malleys; a transition period, 1968–1980, when the theatre underwent the teething difficulties commensurate with a move from a private to a public theatre company; and the period 1981 to the present, when the involvement of the O'Malleys ended and the theatre began to consolidate its position as the main repertory theatre in the north of Ireland.

Origins: 1951–1968

The Lyric Players Theatre originated in 1950 with a Christmas entertainment for the Newman Society of Queen's University Belfast. Directed by Mary O'Malley, it proved sufficiently successful that the group decided to keep the company going at Ulsterville House, the home of Mrs. O'Malley and her husband Pearse, a doctor:

> The consulting room at Ulsterville House was our auditorium, and the window recess our stage. It was a stage that demanded a strong nerve, iron discipline and very neat footwork if you hoped to avoid being catapulted into the arms of the audience.[145]

Such difficulties were caused by the fact that the stage and auditorium were on one level, only divided by a trough of footlights. Further lighting was very simply provided by two spotlights on tripods and a lantern with an assortment of coloured filters. In such confined space, one-act plays were the obvious choice to most of the players; O'Malley, however, 'personally thought of verse plays'[146] and staged Robert Farren's verse play, *Lost Light*, as the company's first production. The players went on to present works by Yeats, Clarke and Valentin Iremonger for audiences of about 25 people in the drawing-room theatre. The name, The Lyric Players Theatre, was chosen 'to associate with, but be distinct from Austin Clarke's Lyric Theatre in Dublin which had a similar policy.'[147] The audience was an invited one: there was no charge for 'admission or for programmes or even a cover charge for the posting of invitations'.[148] This principle of non-payment would continue until March 1960, when the theatre was converted into a non-profit-making Association.

In 1952 the O'Malleys moved to a new house at Derryvolgie Avenue where a narrow loft, which had formerly been part of the stables, was converted into a small theatre. There the tiny stage measured just ten feet by twelve feet, 'actually smaller than the drawing-room recess in Lisburn Road; the auditorium was 10 by 30.'[149] Nonetheless, for the first production, *Icaro* by Lauro de Bosis, O'Malley managed to put a cast of 22 on the stage, admitting only that 'much ingenuity was needed to manoeuvre the cast'.[150] By 1956, this small space had hosted thirty-two productions: 16 were Irish, three were Greek, seven were English and the remaining five were American, Russian, Spanish, Italian and Chinese.[151] John Boyle, an early associate of the company, frankly evaluated the work:

> 'A positive gain has been the chance of seeing the work of dramatists shunned by the commercial theatre... and presented rarely even by specialist societies. More debatable is the value of performing 'straight' versions of Elizabethan plays requiring in particular a depth not available on a small stage. Occasionally, too, the theatre has been ill-served by translations... productions may have irritated, bewildered or impressed me, but they have not left me apathetic...'[152]

The company continued to present a challenging repertoire, and reviews were in general good, not only locally but nationally. A policy was rapidly established that

> 'Neither the physical limitations of the stage nor the inherent difficulties of a play were to be decisive in preventing a production... It would be idle to pretend that success was the inevitable result. There were times... when a bigger stage would have allowed a more willing suspension of disbelief in some of the scenes. Yet... there were other productions that triumphed over the constrictions imposed by finite space.'[153]

Simultaneously, the Lyric Players continued to branch out into other areas of the arts. Poetry recitals and lectures had begun in 1951, while exhibitions of paintings, photographs and sculptures were organised from 1954. In autumn 1956 the Drama School was founded. Providing structured classes in movement and dance, voice and speech training, and acting, over the years it became an important feature of the company. In 1957 a literary magazine, *Threshold*, was also founded in order to 'let the world know what we were up to'.[154] Edited until 1961 by Mary O'Malley, it was intermittently produced thereafter under the changing editorship of writers such as Seamus Heaney, John Montague, John Boyd, Roy McFadden and Patrick Galvin.

As a result of this activity, however, the O'Malleys eventually decided that the 'spill-over into the house was disruptive'.[155] Hence, in 1957 an extension was built to make the theatre self-contained; for the first time, there was proper foyer and dressing room accommodation, and a large supper room and coffee-making area. By now, a discernible style in the work of the company was being recognised as 'actors and artists who had worked closely together during this period were beginning to evolve a group style of acting'.[156] In 1959 this style was acclaimed when the Lyric Players featured as part of the Dublin International Theatre Festival, presenting *Oedipus at Colonus and The Death of Cuchulain* at the Dagg Hall, Westland Row. However, as the scope of the theatre's work increased, it became commensurately difficult to manage. The principle of private theatricals was proving more and more complex to operate, and soon, the company had reached an impasse:

> 'Financially, the subsidy, provided privately, was no longer sufficient. Artistically, the limitations of the small theatre would soon be a handicap and the organisation of such a theatre was no longer a job for one or two individuals.'[157]

Hence, in 1960 the decision was taken to establish the Lyric Players as a non-profit making association. Under this arrangement, the O'Malleys would continue to support the company's practical requirements (accommodation, heating and light etc.) for the present, but the theatre would henceforth come under the control of a voluntary Board of Trustees. At an Inaugural Dinner on March 1 1960, the first Board was named as Deborah Brown, Terence Flanagan, John Hewitt, Denis Johnston, Gabriel Fallon, Pearse O'Malley and Mary O'Malley. To them would be entrusted the objective

'To present plays of cultural and educational value from world theatre which shall in each year include one play by William Butler Yeats and in the selection of which special consideration shall be given to the work of Irish poets, writers and dramatists...'

Other duties included 'the task of managing all the affairs of the Association, continuing the existing policy of the theatre, and providing a new building with better facilities for staging productions as well as encouraging the development of the complementary activities.'[158]

Of these, the undertaking to build a new theatre was the most daunting and ambitious. A young Dublin architect, Neil Downes, had designed a model of the proposed building in time for the Inaugural Dinner; this was to be built in two phases. Sorting practical details and raising the money to erect the theatre would not prove easy. Only in June 1965 was a site found, and even then, while the location (at the end of Ridgeway Street and overlooking the river) was suitable, the space was 'hardly adequate. Having no other option, we decided to go ahead.'[159]

The Foundation Stone for the new theatre was laid on June 12, 1965 by Austin Clarke. Immediately afterwards a feasibility study was commissioned by the company, which set a fund-raising target of £110,000. Despite intense activity, raising the money required was proving problematic. Negotiations took place with the Arts Council of Northern Ireland, and the theatre plan was revised. The Lyric agreed to build a theatre to seat 300, rather than the 197 of the original plans; the Arts Council then provided a grant towards the project of £20,000.[160] This was to be utilised between April 1967 and March 1968. In November 1967 it was decided to begin building on the basis of the resources available. Neil Downes resigned as the theatre's architect and as trustee, and the design finally used was by Frank Wright.[161]

Meanwhile, artistic activity at the theatre had continued to expand further. An Irish Handcrafts shop, intended to help subsidise the theatre undertakings, was opened on June 21, 1962 at premises in Grosvenor Road. This location would also provide space for an office, the Drama School, and for the New Gallery, launched in 1963. That same year an Academy of Music was also founded, and in 1968 the amalgamated Academy of Music and Drama moved to new premises at Cromwell Road. The theatrical aspect of the Lyric's work was no less busy. The company performed at the first Yeats Summer School in 1960, and undertook subsequent visits in 1961 and 1962. It also returned to the Dublin International Theatre Festival in 1960 and 1961. A formal corps of players was formed in 1961 which was intended to partake in a certain number of productions each year. This included Joan Carslake, Sheelagh Garvin, Alice Berger Hammerschlag, Kathleen Kelly, Birgit Kirkpatrick, Helen Lewis, George Mooney, Babs Mooney, Sam McCready, Olga McKeown and Louis Rolston. In an experiment to utilise other, larger spaces on occasion, nine productions were undertaken at the Grove Theatre between 1965 and 1968: *The Heart's a Wonder, The Field, Who's Afraid of Virginia Woolf, Shadow of a Gunman, The Chair, Juno and the Paycock, The Plough and the Stars,*

The Last Eleven and All Soul's Night. The O'Casey plays proved particularly successful. Meanwhile, the company's reputation for Yeats productions was consolidated by reviews such as that from the *Irish Times* of June 1965:

> 'Once again this company and their astonishing director-producer, Mrs. Mary O'Malley, expand the tiny space in which they operate and so enlarge the spirit that the fearsome tensions, the exaltation and the mystery of the Yeatsian drama are not merely communicated, but experienced...'[162]

The company seemed ready for its move to Ridgeway Street. Its last performance at Derryvolgie Avenue, Yeats's *Resurrection*, took place in June 1968.

1968–1980

The 'New Lyric Players Theatre' opened on October 26, 1968 with Christopher Fitz-Simon as the new Director of Productions. Mary O'Malley had decided to resign her day-to-day theatre duties in August 1968, and became instead an unpaid artistic advisor to the trustees. The four Yeats plays of the Cuchulain cycle, directed by Mary O'Malley, were the first productions at the new theatre. These were well received, the *London Observer* critic writing that the company 'know the plays so intimately, and are sufficiently trained as dancers, that they impose both the pace and abstraction as music does...'

Once opening night was over, however, a troubled period for the company began. Just three days after the theatre's opening, both Mary and Pearse O'Malley abruptly resigned as board members. The issue, an on-going one, was the playing of the National Anthem after performances. The O'Malleys believed its playing 'would affect artistic independence and vision',[163] and as a consequence the National Anthem had not been played at Derryvolgie Avenue. The decision was a controversial one, and had resulted, it was felt by the Trustees, in an 'erroneous impression'[164] of the Lyric at a time of on-going fundraising. To counteract this, it was suggested that a policy on the playing of the National Anthem be adopted. O'Malley says 'A split vote was recorded to play the Anthem on 28 October',[165] and O'Malley and her husband resigned as a consequence. In response, the Board requested that the O'Malleys re-think their resignation, and Pearse O'Malley returned to the Board.

Nevertheless, the theatre's troubles continued. A letter in March 1969 to Lyric members from the theatre trustees described the theatre's current 'difficult transition from a small and personal 'little' theatre to a full-time public Theatre, playing regularly to a wider audience'. The trustees had decided that they

> 'were carrying too much staff. We felt the best way to put matters right was to have a temporary break in productions, terminate all contracts and re-advertise posts within a new and tighter organisation.'

There were also, they decided, problems with management, and with 'integrating full-time Professionals and Professional players available only at intervals'.[166] The theatre closed for re-organisation after its January 1969 production of *Royal Hunt of the Sun*. It re-opened after two weeks with Denis Smyth as Director of Productions, Fitz-Simon having resigned before the structural changes. Soon afterwards, in June, it was decided by the Board to close the Grosvenor Road premises, and with it the Irish Handcrafts and New Gallery.

The company carried on despite its debts until the end of 1969, when more trouble flared. A fund-raising group, established at the invitation of the theatre's former chairman Mr. Frank Benner, prepared a fund-raising document for signing by the trustees to 'place beyond any doubt that the theatre is non-political'.[167] The document included an item stating that the playing of the National Anthem was accepted as part of the ceremonial involved on special official and public occasions. Though O'Malley described this as innocuous enough in itself, he declined to sign and in a statement said that 'the method of presentation and the background were such that no self-respecting individual could have anything to do with it.'[168] Four of the seven trustees of the theatre resigned shortly afterwards, stating that 'in view of Dr. O'Malley's lack of co-operation in this matter... they could no longer accept responsibility for the theatre's affairs'.[169] As the Arts Council could only pay grants to a legally constituted authority, three new trustees were appointed on December 15, 1969: Mr. Charles Carville, Dr. Colm Kelly and Mrs. O'Malley.[170] 'Everyone will hope', commented the Annual Report of the Arts Council of Northern Ireland, 'that the theatre is moving into a more stable period... Fortunately difficulties in the theatre's board room have not been allowed to interfere with the quality of the product...'[171]

With the theatre facing continuing financial difficulty, compounded by the considerable publicity surrounding recent events, O'Malley re-assumed day-to-day running of the theatre. She continued in this capacity until June 1976 when she 'tendered my resignation as Trustee and Artistic Adviser'.[172] Over the next decade, and despite the major civil disturbances, the company began to consolidate its position. The Yeats play was still performed annually, but as part of programmes which included classics such as Arthur Miller's *Death of a Salesman* and Goldsmith's *She Stoops to Conquer*. Musicals were also staged, and in 1974, though religious protests took place outside the theatre, over 15,000 people attended *Jesus Christ Superstar*. New writing also featured, and the company developed particularly strong links with local writers John Boyd and Patrick Galvin. Boyd's *The Flats* and Galvin's *We Do it for Love* were especially successful, the latter breaking all box-office records and touring by invitation to Glasgow, Clwyd, Manchester, London, Dublin and Cork. In 1975–6, to mark its twenty-fifth anniversary, the company presented an unbroken sequence of Irish plays, *From Farquhar to Friel*, which was very well supported.

This work was undertaken despite the Troubles, when reports stated that 'attendances at most theatres have been affected by the disturbances in the Province'.[173] The Lyric was the only theatre in Belfast to remain open throughout 1971–1972. During the Worker's Strike

'There were continuous power cuts and almost everything had closed down apart from ourselves. The theatre was frequently plunged into darkness without notice, but we were ready; tilly lamps were laid on... Heating was a problem since this was dependent on electricity, so we tried to heat the place with Kosengas heaters before the audience came, removing them when the show started.'[174]

Though there were occasional bomb blasts in the area, the theatre escaped damage, and in fact began to extend its premises. During the 1976 tour extensions were made to the stage and dressing room areas, while purchases were also made over this period of land adjoining the theatre, and of houses near the building for wardrobe, props, furniture, extra Green Room facilities and office premises. As a result, and though grants from the Arts Council steadily increased, the company was 'stretched to the limit' financially between 1975 and 1977, but managed to avoid a crisis.[175] There was controversy, too, with Equity, the actors' union, which would provide only two new union cards per year as, it stated, there were sixteen thousand actors and actresses out of work in the British Isles. O'Malley thought this 'no consolation', and in a letter to the *Belfast Telegraph* responded that

'The Lyric, in providing Irish and world theatre, depends for its real character and survival on local involvement. It is, accordingly, of the highest importance that as many local actors as possible be employed, and, indeed, it seems quite absurd that a theatre subsidised by this community cannot employ people from within the community.'[176]

This, combined with funding difficulties and the nature of the old Lyric, which mixed professional and amateur performers, made it difficult for the original company ideal to survive. Once the group left Derryvolgie, there was never again to be a Lyric company in the sense understood in the early years. O'Malley herself resigned in 1976, but accepted an invitation to act as an Honorary Director. Pearse O'Malley continued as Honorary Secretary to the Board until 1980; while he remained as a Trustee thereafter, he 'no longer retained a major influence in the running of the theatre.'[177] The transition period had ended; the Lyric was now over ten years at Ridgeway Street. It issued a special publication, *The Needle's Eye*, to mark the event, wherein it was stated that

'it was an outrageous ambition to create such a theatre in the first place... It took the vision, the fierce will, and let it be recorded, much of the personal income of the O'Malleys to bring it from conception through the early days of a private theatre into the public arena. Their almost jealous nurturing of the first ten public years, with the potentially destructive blessing of massive public grants, has ensured that a tradition has begun: a tradition of high standards in a poets' theatre subsidised by the Arts Council...'[178]

1980–present

The Lyric Players Theatre is now the 'Province's only professional company operating all the year round in a purpose-built theatre'.[179] After the departure of Mary O'Malley, it began a now established pattern of employing Artistic Directors to the company on a contractual basis. These have included Tony Diner, Michael Poynor, Sam McCready, Leon Rubin, Patrick Sanford, Richard Digby-Day, Tom Jordan, Roland Jaquerello, Charlie Nowieselski and the present Artistic Director, Robin Midgely. While the theatre has been very much shaped by their individual contributions, sometimes controversially, overall they have tended to continue the mixed programming begun in the 1970s, combining world and Irish classics, contemporary drama, musicals, Christmas shows and new writing. There is 'a more discernible emphasis on local drama, both old and new, and fewer productions of Yeats [have] resulted'.[180] Such local drama includes new work by playwrights such as Jennifer Johnston, Eugene McCabe, Graham Reid, Robin Glendinning, Christina Reid, John Boyd, Wilson John Haire and Martin Lynch. Some of this work has been very successful, and a number of these plays have 'contributed to the growing Belfast tradition of social realism',[181] notable examples in this being Lynch's *Dockers* and Graham Reid's *The Hidden Curriculum*.

Financial difficulties have, at times, re-surfaced. In the late 1980s, problems arose when 'lower than anticipated box-office income allied [to] persistent under-funding in previous years led to a crisis.'[182] The theatre was closed on April 1, 1987 to give time for forward planning, and it re-opened in autumn of that year with Hugh Leonard's *Da*, which was a box-office success. By 1989, however, the Lyric was again facing a mounting deficit and programme revisions were made. Nevertheless, the company had accumulated a 'significant deficit',[183] and in 1990 the Board of Trustees adopted a three-year business plan aimed at 'eliminating the theatre's debts and gradually increasing the production budgets'.[184] Targets were gradually met, and the theatre moved towards a period of financial stability. In 1993 a revised constitution was put in place, with 'new arrangements for the governance of the theatre', and another three-year plan adopted. In the Arts Council Report for 1993/4, it was stated that

'the recently appointed management team at the Lyric Theatre – the province's only repertory company – has already embraced the new [regional theatre] concept by promoting the accessibility of the theatre to the public, planning to stay open during the summer months, and by collaborating with local professional companies and inviting them to perform on the Lyric stage. It is of paramount importance to the theatre to ensure that there is a place in the dramatic repertoire for the authentic voice of the people of the province.'[185]

Co-productions have since been undertaken with Tinderbox on *Galloping Buck Jones*, and with Point Fields on *Lengthening Shadows*. While continuing its own productions, the Lyric has also been made available to other groups, including, for example, regional showcases of the BT National Connections youth theatre festival and amateur drama festivals. The Lyric has also undertaken more touring productions. Notable successes in the recent past have included the Lyric's production of Brian Friel's *Philadelphia, Here I Come!* which travelled to the United States. The Lyric Studio was launched in 1997, with a production of Friedrich Durrenmatt's *The Visit*, reviving the concept of the earlier Lyric Studio which had produced Peter Weiss' *Marat-Sade* in 1980 under the guidance of Sam McCready. Meanwhile, the Youth Lyric continues the earlier emphasis of the company on the training of young people, with summer musicals also placing a strong emphasis on youth participation. The Lyric Theatre is unusual in that it has consistently recorded its activities for archival purposes, and holds a considerable amount of material at the theatre itself.

(Full production list in archive catalogue)

Grove Theatre, Belfast (1965–[1978])

The Grove Theatre opened on October 4, 1965 at the Shore Road, Belfast. Formerly the Troxy Cinema, it had been renovated and redecorated by the management of the cinema together with the Arts Council of Northern Ireland. The two organisations shared the cost of renovation; in return the building remained the property of the original management, while the Arts Council received limited degrees of priority in rental of the theatre for its own presentations.[186] In practice, this meant the management was committed to present Council-backed productions for a minimum period annually, with other companies free to negotiate use of the theatre during the remainder of the year.[187] The new theatre was a large-scale one. It had a depth of stage of 17 feet 16 inches, which could be increased by means of a 100 foot apron, and seated about 1200 people.[189] Its first five-week season 'opened auspiciously'[190] with Harold Goldblatt's Ulster Theatre Company appearing in *The Old Broom* by George Shiels. This was followed by two visiting companies, York Promotions Ltd. with *The Game* by Alun Owens, and Westminster Theatre Company's *Mr. Wilberforce M.P.* by Alan Thornhill. Micheal MacLiammoir appeared in the week of October 25 with his show, *Talking About Yeats*, and the season was rounded off by the Lyric Theatre's production of *The Heart's a Wonder*, Nuala and Mairin O'Farrell's adaptation of Synge's *The Playboy of the Western World*. Though the concept of the Grove was welcomed, the building was quickly criticised. Mary O'Malley, who directed a number of Lyric Theatre productions at the theatre, thought the Grove 'even after renovation, a large uncomfortable building with poor acoustics' and deemed its stage 'inflexible'.[191] Critics too complained of 'poor acoustics in the Grove', and reported that 'one feels at times as if one were looking at a television play with the sound not properly turned up'.[192] Nevertheless, the theatre was booked by other companies for the period after the Arts Council season, first for variety and then pantomime. *Dick Whittington* opened well, but was forced to close a week early. The theatre manager, Mr. E. Watson, stated that this was simply 'a question of the situation of the Grove and the fact that the theatre is not well known'.[193]

Other productions therefore continued, with performances of Indian and Spanish dance, and a première of Stuart Love's *The Big Long Bender* by Anglo-Irish Productions with a cast which included Bill Morrisson, Stephen Rea and Sian Davis. The well-established and respected amateur Circle Theatre staged productions at the new theatre. Variety, too, became a regular feature; critic Graham McKenzie stated that

'it took me back to those little shows we used to attend in the village hall. The standard was higher at the Grove but the atmosphere was the same... people are actually going to variety shows. The well-filled car park at the Grove was evidence of this. And they were regaled by an enjoyable, if somewhat predictable programme reminiscent of the heyday of the Empire...'[194]

However, by September the theatre was again in difficulty. It was reported that there was good entertainment at the theatre, but 'a minimum of people and a consequent lack of any theatrical atmosphere'.[195] Management confessed that except for shows with very well-known performers, 'we just did not draw the crowd. Yet when we forsook the clean, quality show last summer for a series of X Certificate films, the theatre was absolutely packed.'[196]

Despite this, the Arts Council was determined 'to establish a continuing policy over a period, even if it means opening a season on a limited budget and going on only so long as public support makes it possible'.[197] Hence, in 1967 it undertook an extensive programme of alteration to improve the acoustics of the theatre, now generally agreed to be unsatisfactory. By its annual report for 1966/7, it was stated that audiences for Arts Council supported shows had been

'growing steadily over the years that the Council has been working there in the most amicable partnership with the owners, and the proportion of straight theatre to other entertainment has been increasing too... there is scope for development at the Grove, and this will be pursued...'[198]

In 1964/5 the theatre had presented five weeks of live theatre; in 1965/6 there was a thirteen-week season, not including circus, variety or pantomime. By 1967/8 the figure had risen to seventeen weeks of live theatre. Arts Council events at the theatre tended to involve high-profile companies. The 1968 programme, for example, included performances by the Royal Shakespeare Company's Theatre-go-Round, the Royal Ballet, the Abbey Theatre and Prospect Productions of Cambridge, and excellent houses were recorded for some of these events. In 1969, two major theatre events were planned: a version of George Shiels' *Macook's Corner* by the Ulster Theatre Company directed by Tyrone Guthrie, and a production of *Hadrian VII* by Peter Luke, organised by Harold Goldblatt in a co-production with the Abbey Theatre. The former, reported the Arts Council, was 'something of a landmark',[199] warmly received in Belfast and transferring to Dublin and Cork. However,

Hadrian VII was less successful. Four bomb scares occurred during its run, and despite being a 'fine production', it recorded 'one of the lowest audience responses in all the five years of live theatre at the Grove'.[200] This was the first major intimation of the difficulties which would beset the theatre. Though performances continued, with appearances by some big names such as Josef Locke, audiences figures were poor. In September 1971 the *Belfast Telegraph* reported that 'Belfast's troubles have hit attendances at the Grove theatre... at present the theatre is closed for the summer'.[201] The theatre remained closed until Christmas 1972 when it re-opened with a circus. However, a succession of fires at the theatre, some thought to be malicious, caused damage to the building, and a major fire in July 1977 destroyed a large part of the building. Despite this, the theatre re-opened in December of that year with reduced seating to accommodate 200 people. However, on July 3, 1978 another fire broke out, and on this occasion the damage was extensive. The building does not appear to have been used for theatrical purposes after this date.

Field Day Theatre Company (1980–)

Field Day Theatre Company was founded in 1980 by Stephen Rea and Brian Friel

> '..mainly because Stephen Rea, despite his success on the London stage and in television, wanted to come back to Ireland, to make some contribution to what was happening here. He heard that there might be some money available from the Northern Ireland Arts Council to promote theatre in the province. On an impulse he caught a plane to Belfast and drove to Donegal to see Brian Friel whom he had known since appearing in *The Freedom of the City* at the Royal Court. By what Rea himself describes as 'a magic coincidence', Friel had just completed *Translations*. He was feeling bruised from recent contacts with the professional theatre in London and Dublin and was wondering if he might be able to mount an independent production of his new play. Neither of them had any experience of theatre management when they decided to take a chance, put the play on in Derry and then tour it around Ireland...'[202]

From this somewhat ad hoc beginning came the triumphant opening of *Translations* at Derry's Guildhall, followed by a tour of Ireland north and south and a transfer to London's Royal Court. Acclaimed by both critics and public alike, this play was to prove the first of a series of controversial and challenging works premièred by the company. These include not only plays, but also a series of pamphlets and most recently, *The Field Day Anthology of Irish Writing*. Of the plays, Thomas Kilroy's *Double Cross* (1986) and Stewart Parker's *Pentecost* (1987) were particularly successful, and exemplified the aims of the aims of the company as outlined in 1981:

> 'firstly, to forge a Northern-based theatre company which would rehearse and tour in the North and then tour throughout the whole of

Ireland; secondly, to concentrate on smaller venues, where theatre is rarely seen; and finally, to perform plays of excellence in a distinctively Irish voice that would be heard throughout the whole of Ireland.'[203]

Field Day has appeared in towns and villages all over the island. The company has deliberately remained a non-building based enterprise, and the company of performers has always been an impermanent one, differing from show to show. However, Field Day has continued the method of working established with *Translations*, rehearsing and premièring its plays in Derry, and then touring extensively throughout the island. The 1984 productions, for example, were seen in Derry, Dublin, Belfast, Carrickmore, Enniskillen, Magherafelt, Downpatrick, Armagh, Newry, Mullingar, Athlone, Galway, Ballycastle, Limavady, Coleraine, Limerick and Cork. Such shows were well supported; in 1990 the Arts Council of Northern Ireland reported that Field Day had

'a strong following and in 1989 drew average attendances of 71% capacity for its twelve-week tour when it gave fifty-five performances of *Saint Oscar* by Terry Eagleton in twenty-two venues...'

Despite going on to praise the 'consistently high' production standards of the company, the report also notes the 'inevitable difficulties associated with a long tour involving one-night stands'.[204] This serves as a reminder that, on one level, Field Day has very much been a practical touring theatre company, struggling with the typical day-to-day problems of funding, administration, commissioning and so on. The company has often used large casts, in one case fourteen people, who were on the road for two to three months and played at many small venues. Hence, and despite support from various organisations such as the Arts Councils north and south, Derry City Council, and the Northern Ireland Tourist Board, finance has always been a problem.[205]

Nonetheless, Field Day has also existed on another level. In 1981, a Board of Directors was formally announced, consisting of Friel, Rea, David Hammond, Seamus Heaney, Seamus Deane and Tom Paulin. In 1983 the company began publishing pamphlets, the first set written by three of the new directors: *A New Look at the Language Question* by Tom Paulin, *An Open Letter* by Seamus Heaney, and *Civilians and Barbarians* by Seamus Deane. These were intended to

'contribute to the solution of the present crisis by producing analyses of the established opinions, myths and stereotypes which [have] become both a symptom and a cause of the current situation.'[206]

Like some others to follow, the first pamphlets caused considerable controversy and received a stormy reception in intellectual circles. This focused on the fact that in the opinion of some critics, as summarised by Eavan Boland, these first pamphlets were promoting 'green nationalism and divided culture'. [207] In contrast, Mary Holland wrote in a piece on *Field Day's Tenth Birthday* for the *Cure at Troy* programme, that

'This taunt seems to me to ignore the efforts which Field Day has made to embrace a more inclusive concept of what it means to be Irish... to make it possible to talk about nationalism without seeming to pose a threat to others.'[208]

In the only full-length analysis of the company published to date, Marilynn J. Richtarik argues that the relationship between these controversial pamphlets and the on-the-ground theatrical venture was 'the most basic fault line' of the company.[209] The connection between them, she believes, remained largely undefined, and this meant the Field Day productions were increasingly perceived and reviewed in a political context created by the pamphlets. Conversely, in his evaluation of the work of the company for *Theatre Ireland*, Paul Hadfield thought

'the effect of the division, not to say diversification, of Field Day's operational focus has had a broadly positive effect on the company's public profile, without necessarily adding to the pre-existing clarity of what the company stands for. There is a sense in which this philosophical opaqueness has added to the resonance and allusiveness in the company's professed aims.'[210]

However, he agreed that difficulties also existed with the publishing aspect of the company, most crucially the fact that it 'has obscured the company's founding purpose (and the function for which it is still best known in these islands) – to take new plays for audiences unused to going to the theatre.'[211]

Field Day has been a company of undoubted significance in the Irish theatre. Hadfield concludes his piece by stating that any definite decision to close the company, which had an uncertain future at his time of writing, would leave a gap 'that will be hard, not to say impossible, for others to fill'.[212] Likewise, Richtarik concludes that the Field Day project has had aspects which make it unique:

'the interplay between local circumstances, political compromises, financial restrains, and personalities that finally make it possible to talk about 'a Field Day play' rather than simply 'a play Field Day has done.'[213]

For Anthony Roche in *Contemporary Irish Drama*, 'The dramatic qualities of most of the plays it commissioned remain Field Day's greatest strength and legacy'.[214] However, while the Field Day company has not had a production since 1995, it has temporarily suspended its theatrical activity rather than disbanded. Its production list to date is as follows: *Translations* by Brian Friel (1980); *Three Sisters* by Anton Chekhov, version by Brian Friel (1981); *The Communication Cord* by Brian Friel (1982); *Boesman and Lena* by Athol Fugard (1983); *The Riot Act* by Tom Paulin, after Sophocles' *Antigone* and *High Time* by Derek Mahon, after Molière's *L'Ecole des Maris* (1984); *Double Cross* by Thomas Kilroy (1986); *Pentecost* by Stewart Parker (1987); *Making History* by Brian Friel (1988); *Saint Oscar* by Terry Eagleton (1989); *The Cure at Troy* by Seamus Heaney, after Sophocles' *Philoctetes* (1990); *The Madame Macadam*

Travelling Theatre by Thomas Kilroy (1991); *Cries from Casement as his Bones are Brought to Dublin* by David Rudkin (playreading, 1992); *Uncle Vanya* by Anton Chekhov, version by Frank McGuinness (1995).
(Full production list in archive catalogue)

Charabanc Theatre Company (1983–1995)

Founded by five Belfast actresses in 1983, Charabanc Theatre Company became one of the foremost Irish theatre companies during its subsequent twelve-year history. Born of frustration at the scarcity of work for women in theatre, and at the nature of the work which was available to them, the company channelled its energies into originating new theatre work. The resultant plays

> 'explored ways of dealing with the lives of 'insignificant' people, women who are supposed to have no place in history other than as extras for the crowd scenes. They [have] forged a kind of wit and fluidity that allows them to deal with oppression without being oppressive, with boredom without being boring, confinement without being confined... assurance is brought to bear in keeping the balance between enlightenment and entertainment that the material demands.'[215]

From the first, Charabanc established a notable working method and ethos. 'Working – or mostly not working – in the theatre here',[216] actresses Eleanor Methven, Marie Jones, Carol Scanlan, Brenda Winter and Maureen McAuley decided to stage their own production in 1983. Local playwright Martin Lynch convinced them that they should write their own play about Belfast women, and a process began which would become a habitual way of working for the company. After researching archive sources, 'history books, old newspaper cuttings and newsreel',[217]

> 'we go and interview people about the subject matter... We were talking to people, not just about working in mills or being involved in the 1949 election, but about the attitude of the time. We spoke to teachers, doctors, ministers, and people from all walks of life to get a clear idea. We had all these tapes and interviews...[218] [Then] we go away to a place called Annaghmakerrig, which is Tyrone Guthrie's house... we actually sit down with all those tapes and listen to them again...We generally have an idea of what the play is going to be about. We talk about it and try to put in the story line. We talk about the characters – where they come from and who they are. Then we try to work out a story board and work the characters into the scenes.'[219]

Marie Jones would then undertake the actual writing, with the drafts undergoing a collective editing process. This could be on-going:

> 'We'd keep an ending for a week or two and then we'd change it again. Because we're writing our own stuff it's never finished. We're always striving to make it better – to perfect it. It's a good opportunity that actors don't normally get.'[220]

As a result, Charabanc's initial plays were 'collaborative work in which author-
ship was difficult to pinpoint'.[221] The first, *Lay Up Your Ends*, was credited to
Martin Lynch, Marie Jones and the company, and proved an instant critical
and popular success. Set in York Street Linen Mill, Belfast, it was based on the
two-week strike of the (mostly female) Belfast Linen Workers in 1911. Using
minimal set and props, the drama was directed by Pam Brighton and featured
a style which would become characteristic of Charabanc's earlier work, with

> 'rapid-fire narrative, short sharp scenes, plentiful wit, commentary and
> song, reflecting the public and private experience of the workers'.[222]

The play opened at the Arts Theatre, Belfast on May 15, 1983 'to the unfamiliar sight of hundreds of people queuing right down Botanic Avenue'.[223]
By the following October, it had been seen by 13,515 people in 96 performances in 59 different venues. The company was credited with having rapidly
carved out

> 'a new and comprehensive touring circuit that included both rural and
> urban venues... Audiences ranged from farmers and ex-mill women to
> the arts festival crowds. The appeal to a broader base, one which includes
> the working-classes, became a priority in the company's work'.[224]

Originally, the Charabanc members had intended to revert to their original
paths after one production. The success of *Lay Up Your Ends*, however, convinced some of the actresses to carry on, and a core company emerged of
Methven, Scanlan and Jones. Between 1983 and 1988 they worked with directors Pam Brighton, Ian McElhinney, Andy Hinds and Peter Sheridan to stage
six new plays to acclaim: *Oul Delf and False Teeth* (1984); *Now You're Talkin'*
(1985); *Gold in the Streets* (1986); *The Girls in the Big Picture* (1986); and
Somewhere Over the Balcony (1987). All of these were devised by the company,
but Jones' responsibility for the final writing process was reflected in her full
billing as the writer of the plays from *The Girls in the Big Picture* onwards. The
subject matters covered were quite diverse. *Oul Delf and False Teeth* was set in
the Markets area during the 1949 Stormont elections, while *Now You're Talkin'*
was a contemporary piece set in a centre for the reconciliation of sectarian
conflict. *Gold in the Streets* dealt with the theme of Irish emigration to England
over the twentieth century. The claustrophobia, social pressures and prejudices
of village life in rural Ulster of the 1960s were explored in *The Girls in the Big
Picture*, while *Somewhere Over the Balcony* featured life in Belfast's Divis Flats on
the eve of the anniversary of the introduction of internment.
    Though reviews of these productions were not without criticism, the bal-
ance of individual reviews was overwhelmingly positive. *Fortnight's* review of
The Girls in the Big Picture typifies the critical response:

> 'Somebody, perhaps the director, should cut the dead wood from this
> production... On the other hand many smoother professional companies
> must long for the human interest of Charabanc scripts and the honest,
> sensitive, gritty, explosive acting of the principals'.[225]

Common to all Charabanc reviews are references to a 'pithy and dark and incisively unsentimental'[226] humour, and to ensemble playing wherein 'a nod is not just as good as a wink but as a whole speech'.[227] Both of these elements were tested in the considerable amount of overseas touring undertaken by the company. As momentum at home built up, the company began to accept invitations from festivals and theatres abroad. Plays were staged at Mayfest, Glasgow 1984; the International Theatre Festival, Munich; the Dublin Theatre Festival; the Edinburgh Theatre Festival; the du Maurier World Stage Festival, Toronto, Canada; and at a range of festivals in the USA. A tour was undertaken in 1984 to Moscow, Leningrad, and Vilnius; the company also travelled regularly to perform in London. Again, the critical and popular responses were extremely positive, and the frequently recorded difficulties with accent and idiom were rapidly overcome:

'...it's worth missing the odd joke beneath the broad accents, when the final product gives so strong a flavour of a fascinating lost community.'[228]

By 1988, however, the core members of the company had 'reached a point of creative exhaustion'.[229] There were also perennial financial difficulties, and Charabanc was 'chronically short of funds'.[230] As the company received funding on a project-by-project basis from the Arts Council, company members were paid solely for performance work. This meant that their essential, extensive research time went unpaid. Difficulties had also arisen with funding for community tours, with the company stating:

'It seems crazy that because of financial cuts we are no longer able to play the community centres, which is, after all, where our real audiences are. We feel we are being pushed out of our own ground and what is the point of performing half way around the world if we can't play to the people on our own doorstep... the people our plays are actually about?'[231]

Though the community funding situation would eventually be rectified, there began for the members 'an eighteen-month transition period, six months of which was spent working apart on individual projects'.[232] For the first time, Charabanc sought scripts by outside writers, ideally featuring different cultural backgrounds pertinent to their own. This was felt by the Artistic Directors to be 'a way of relieving some of the pressure',[233] and 'a necessary and healthy process'.[234] Two successful productions resulted on this basis in 1989: *The Stick Wife* by American writer Darragh Cloud explored the lives of Klan wives in Alabama in the 1960s, while *Cauterised* by Neill Speers focused on two women working in an old-fashioned hardware store in rural Northern Ireland.

Meanwhile, Charabanc also produced two short pieces by Jones, *The Terrible Twins' Crazy Christmas*, commissioned by the Riverside Theatre, Coleraine in 1988, and *Weddin's, Wee'ins and Wakes*, an examination of the Protestant culture in Belfast which was first performed at the 1989 Shankill Festival. Like the *Stick Wife, Cauterised* and *The Terrible Twins*, the production combined outside actors with some core members. Not until *The Hamster Wheel* in 1990 did the entire company come together again to stage a play based on long periods of research, and the production, directed by Robert Scanlan, was generally acclaimed. Reviews complimented *The Hamster Wheel* for

> 'imaginatively communicating the true horror of ordinary people trying to find the courage to cope with overwhelming events'.[235]

The increasing consolidation of the company's position was also reflected in frequent references to a 'Charabanc tradition'[236] and a Charabanc 'philosophy'.[237] A dissenting voice was, however, heard in *Theatre Ireland*. Pam Brighton, a former director with Charabanc, made a range of criticisms in her assessment of the company for the magazine. These included a suggestion that in recent productions the company was moving away from 'everything Charabanc had set out to do'.[238] A stout rebuttal was issued by the Board of Directors of Charabanc in the following edition of the magazine, stressing the fact that

> 'a company's artistic development is an ongoing process of diversification and growth... Charabanc Theatre Company has of course developed and diversified greatly since 1985... whilst continually having its own community as a touchstone.'[239]

In the wider context, this debate served to highlight the fact that Charabanc was moving into a new phase in its work, which would take it 'in new formal and stylistic directions'.[240] Though the company jointly presented *Weddin's, Wee'ins and Wakes* and *The Blind Fiddler of Glenadauch* by Marie Jones during 1990 and 1991, henceforth Jones would concentrate on her own freelance writing outside the context of the company. Meanwhile, Charabanc's own work continued to diversify into three main strands: devising plays from and for the company's own community, commissioning new Irish writing, and introducing and reinterpreting existing texts. A mission statement noted that for all three

> 'we feel that, within a divided, reactive and conservative society such as ours, the company's contribution must be to confront accepted truths and pose dilemmas... it is still our policy to put women centre stage.'[241]

Extant plays by writers which were subsequently produced included *Me and My Friend* by Gillian Plowman (1991); *Bondagers* by Sue Glover (1991); *Skirmishes* by Catherine Hayes (1992); and *The Vinegar Fly* by Nick Perry (1994). These plays were, in the main, warmly reviewed, and variously described as being 'perfect material for the Charabanc Theatre Company';[242] 'set in the furrow they originally set out to plough';[243] and as having 'Charabanc written all over it in large letters'.[243] For the company's tenth anniversary in 1993, it was decided to undertake adaptations of classic plays. Lynne Parker adapted and directed Lorca's *The House of Bernarda Alba*, setting it 'somewhere in Ireland at some time in the not too distant past'. The production received relatively mixed reviews, but fared better than Peter

Sheridan's adaptation of Corneille's *The Illusion* which followed. This disappointed the critics and the public alike, and the company directors admitted

> 'our tenth anniversary piece wasn't the success we hoped it would be...
> Regardless of who writes a play we produce, we are closely identified
> with the writing because our early plays were written collectively...And
> so we made a very conscious decision that our next major play would
> be new writing, and that it would be given the necessary development
> period.'[245]

New writing had already been undertaken in this diversification period. A short play, *Frontline Café* by Thomas McLaughlin toured the Greater Belfast community centres throughout August 1991; *The Irish Times* thought it 'a masquerade in high style',[246] while *The Guardian* conversely deemed the play 'banal... lacking in subtlety, humour and originality'.[247] A year later, Charabanc was commissioned to produce a play for Derry City's *Impact '92*. *October Song*, a family drama by Andy Hinds centring on the return of a long-lost sister, garnered some reviews which thought it 'vintage Charabanc'[248] but others which were 'rather mixed'.[249] Thomas McLaughlin's play *Iron May Sparkle* did likewise. A 'revue-like riot of comic sketches',[250] it was premièred in London in 1994. Irish reviewers gave the production fulsome praise, but the London critics thought it unsatisfying. Hence, in 1995, Charabanc unveiled a major new writing project. Having spent a year researching the issue of domestic violence, Carol Moore (Scanlan) then worked together with writer Sue Ashby until the final script was ready. Ashby, who taught Creative Writing at Charabanc's major International Workshop Festival in 1993, produced a bleakly ironic play, *A Wife, a Dog and a Maple Tree*. This was deemed 'hard-hitting... and highly theatrical,'[251] and received very positive reviews. Critics thought the play 'struck just the right balance between dramatic impact and highlighting what for many women is a serious problem';[252] the production was deemed to generate

> 'shock currents which penetrate very deeply into the experience of the
> audience, unlocking powerful emotions on either side of the gender
> divide.'[253]

Despite the play's success, it was to prove the last for the company. In July 1995 Charabanc announced that it was to 'get off the bus'. Its two remaining Artistic Directors, Carol Moore and Eleanor Methven, had 'jointly taken the positive decision to pursue separate, independent careers'.[254] One of its final actions was to donate its archives to various institutions, including the Linen Hall Library.

Over its twelve year history, Charabanc's journey had generated an impressive amount of new work. The company was the vanguard for independent touring in Ireland. It brought theatre to diverse new audiences and cleared a path both for the new independent theatre companies, and for companies wishing to work in the area of community drama. The company's story testifies, it has been stated, 'to the popularity of alternative forms of theatre, particularly for audiences who are excluded from or exclude themselves from mainstream or 'high art' theatre'.[255] Given its broader social and political resonances, there have been surprisingly few published analyses of Charabanc's work. This has been attributed by critic Maria DiCenzo to the 'need for academic institutions – teaching, publishing, conferencing – to take seriously the work of companies who function outside the conventional domain of text-based drama'.[256] Nevertheless, Charabanc was described overall by the authoritative *Bloomsbury Theatre Guide* as

> 'versatile and ebullient... the strength of its productions lies in its ability to reveal social networks and loyalties. One of the most entertaining companies to emerge out of Northern Ireland.'

Big Telly Theatre Company, Coleraine (1987–)

Big Telly Theatre Company is Northern Ireland's only permanent professional theatre company based in the regions. Formed in 1987 by three graduates of Kent University, Kate Batts, Jill Holmes, and Zoe Seaton, the company is located at Flowerfield Arts Centre, Portstewart and premières its work at the Riverside Theatre, Coleraine. Since its foundation, Big Telly's programmes have regularly featured plays by writers such as Dario Fo, Eugene Ionesco, John Godber and Steven Berkhoff. These productions have been characterised by a style which incorporates circus, dance, mime and music to create multi-textured pieces of theatre. Led by Artistic Director Zoe Seaton, Big Telly has, however, become best known for creating new theatre works by company members. These include *Onions, I Can See the Sea, Cuchulainn* and *To Hell With Faust*. Contingent on funding, two projects a year travel throughout Ireland. Typically, these include a small-to-middle scale touring production in autumn, an educational project in spring and a community project in summer. The company has strong commitments to arts for young people, taking theatre into both primary and secondary schools in the province. It has also been involved with the local youth theatre since its outset.

Tinderbox Theatre Company (1988–)

Tinderbox was formed in September 1988 when two actors, Tim Loane and Lalor Roddy, decided to create a new company to produce challenging theatre not ordinarily seen in Belfast. They had already previously joined forces to produce two Harold Pinter plays in June 1988; directed by David Grant, these had been presented at the Old Museum Arts Centre to an encouraging response. Hence, under the new name Tinderbox, the company made its first official appearance at the 1988 Belfast Festival at Queen's with Edward Bond's *Stone*, and followed this with a triple bill of Howard Benton plays. Thereafter, while including classic works as part of its brief, Tinderbox has emphasised contemporary writing, and more specifically new work by Irish writers. The company has presented such work at various stages of development, including readings, plays in progress and full productions. This is facilitated by an annual festival of new writing, which was inaugurated in 1989 and has been a joint production with Prime Cut (formerly Mad Cow) Productions since 1996. Some twenty-two scripts have been presented at these *April Sundays* festivals as plays in progress, while a number of plays have been developed from staged readings through to full productions. These include *Fingertips* by Thomas McLaughlin, *Theatre of Paranoia* by Miche Doherty, *Galloping Buck Jones* by Ken Bourke and most notably *Language Roulette* by Daragh Carville which transferred to the Bush Theatre, London in 1997 after an extremely successful Irish tour in 1996. Tinderbox is a non-building based company, and undertakes extensive tours of Ireland both north and south. It has also been involved in co-productions of new plays; with the Lyric Theatre, Belfast on *Galloping Buck Jones* by Ken Bourke, and in the first cross-border co-production, with Pigsback Theatre Company, Dublin on *This Love Thing* by Marina Carr.

(Full production list in archive catalogue).

Replay Productions (1988–)

Replay Productions is Northern Ireland's professional Theatre-in-Education company. Founded in 1988 under the artistic directorship of Brenda Winter, it has aimed to provide both a high quality theatre experience for young people, and a range of learning opportunities for schools. In so doing, Replay has commissioned a considerable amount of new writing, with all but two productions being of original work. Much of Replay's work is written by local playwrights. These have included Gary Mitchell (*That Driving Ambition*, 1995; *Sinking*, 1997); Damian Gorman (*All Being Well*, 1990; *Ground Control to Davy Mental*, 1992; *Stones*, 1994); John Rooney (*Permanent Deadweight*, 1991; *Squinty and the Scotch Giant*, 1994); Marie Jones (*Under Napoleon's Nose*, 1988; *It's a Waste of Time Tracy*, 1989; *The Cow, the Ship and the Indian*, 1991; *Don't Look Down*, 1991; *Yours, Truly*, 1993) and Brenda Winter (*The A Zoo Story*, 1993; *The Great I Am*, 1994; *The Battle for Morrigan's Mound*, 1996). Topics covered by these plays range from the history of Belfast and Irish emigration to alcohol abuse, punishment beatings and refugees. Replay has also created Living History projects on museum and historical sites, the most recent being the 1995 work on life in early times, *Time Hurdlers*, at the Ulster History Park. In that same year, Replay won the BP Arts Award, having already been the recipient of an AIB Better Ireland Award in 1990.

DubbelJoint Productions (1991–)

Formed in 1991 by Pam Brighton, Marie Jones and Mark Lambert, DubbelJoint has the dual aims of creating plays with an appeal throughout the island of Ireland, and making that work as widely available as possible. The name, comprised of Dub (lin) – Bel (fast) Joint, embodies these aims. Pam Brighton has been Artistic Director of the company since its foundation, directing all of its productions to date. Marie Jones has remained the company's Associate Director, while Robert Ballagh has designed most of the company's productions.

DubbelJoint's first production was *Hang All the Harpers*, a historical story of Irish music by Marie Jones and Shane Connaughton which toured Ireland in 1991. *Christmas Eve Can Kill You*, by Marie Jones followed in 1992, and in spring 1993 DubbelJoint premiered Terry Eagleton's *The White, the Gold and the Gangrene*. This controversial piece about the 1916 Easter Rising toured to Dublin, London and throughout Northern Ireland. Later that same year an adaptation by Marie Jones of Gogol's *The Government Inspector* also undertook an Irish tour. This proved extremely successful, and the production transferred to the Tricycle Theatre, London in 1994. Two hugely popular plays succeeded it, and have barely been out of production by DubbelJoint since their respective premières. Staged for the first time at the West Belfast Festival in August 1994, *A Night in November* 'was provoked rather than inspired by'[257] the sectarianism which surrounded the Northern Ireland versus Republic of Ireland World Cup qualifying match in November 1993. Written by Marie Jones and performed by Dan Gordon, this 'funny, moving and provocative'[258] play has to date toured for 50 weeks to 52 different venues including theatres in Dublin, London and New York. It has been seen by in excess of 50,000 people, and won both a TMA/Martini award for Best Regional Touring Production, and a *Belfast Telegraph*/EMA award for Best Actor.[259] *Women on the Verge of HRT* was the company's next production. This tells the story of two forty-something Belfast women who confront a looming mid-life crisis on their weekend pilgrimage to meet Daniel O'Donnell. Like the two previous productions, it opened at the West Belfast Festival in 1995 and became an instant success. It has toured Ireland regularly since, 'bringing a new audience to village halls and metropolitan theatres'[260] and transferred for a season to London's West End in 1997.

Most recently, DubbelJoint staged two new productions by Marie Jones, *Stones in His Pockets* and *Eddie Bottom's Dream*, in 1996. The latter did not, however, prove as successful as the previous productions. The company then embarked on a new venture, co-producing two plays with JustUs Community Theatre from West Belfast. *Just a Prisoner's Wife* was staged by the combination in 1996 at the West Belfast Festival, and won the first Belfast City Council award for Best Arts Partnership. A second co-production, *Binlids*, was produced as part of the 1997 West Belfast Festival. Beginning with the introduction of internment in August 1971, *Binlids* traced the history of the community of the area during the 17 years which followed. The production proved to be contentious, with press accusations that the drama collective had been one-sided in its portrayal of injustice and had 'ignored any facts which might disprove their thesis'.[261] In response, Pam Brighton, who directed the production, stated that the play:

'was not seeking a balance within itself but seeking a balance in the overall perception of what makes West Belfast tick... if the peace process is to gain meaning, this experience has to be understood.'[262]

Binlids has since been invited to tour to New York. A new departure for DubbelJoint will take place in Spring 1998, when it plans to tour Eugene O'Neill's *A Moon for the Misbegotten*.

Prime Cut Productions, Belfast (1992–)
Formerly Mad Cow Productions

Prime Cut Productions was founded (as Mad Cow Productions) in 1992 by four free-lance theatre practitioners working in the Belfast area, Simon Magill, Jackie Doyle, Aidan Lacey and Stuart Marshall. The specific aim of the company was to broaden the repertoire of theatre available in Ireland by producing the work of internationally renowned playwrights yet to be given a local showcase. Plays produced are regularly given Irish tours. Prime Cut has produced Jim Cartwright's *Two* (1992), Athol Fugard's *A Place With the Pigs* (1994), Ariel Dorfman's *Death and the Maiden* (1995) and Sam Shepard's *Simpatico* (1997). In 1994 the company premiered Trevor Griffiths' *Who Shall Be Happy*, which subsequently toured to Denmark, the West Yorkshire Playhouse, and the Bush Theatre to 'positive acclaim'.[263] Prime Cut has also, in recent years, joined with Tinderbox in co-producing Festivals of New Writing, and been nominated for EMA and Belfast City Council arts awards. *(Production list in archive catalogue)*

Independent Companies

In 1993, the annual Arts Council report noted that:

> 'Recent years have seen a remarkable rise in the number of young companies... the productions, style of working and audiences they play to are strikingly diverse.'[264]

Since then, the proliferation of companies 'high in enthusiasm and creative energy who have shown a particular interest in new writing, new styles and new theatre forms'[265] has continued. Such organisations have included Aisling Ghear, the first professional Irish language theatre company, and Centre Stage, which under the guidance of Roma Tomelty and Colin Carnegie regularly produces Ulster classics. Michael Poynor's Ulster Theatre Company has become best-known for its highly successful musicals and pantomimes, while Kabosh has 'lived up to its own trademark 'versatile theatre''.[266] Shanakee Productsions have given contemporary twists to music-hall and variety traditions. Paddy Scully's Belfast Theatre Company produces new and contemporary writing, most recently an adaptation of Brian Moore's *The Feast of Lupercal*. Ridiculusmus have established their initial reputation on their quirky interpretations of the work of Flann O'Brien, while the O'Casey company has devoted itself to presenting the works of Sean O'Casey. Now defunct, Point Fields Theatre company commissioned new plays and organised two festivals of new writing over its six year history from 1990–96. Productions included *Rinty* (1990) and *Pictures of Tomorrow*

77

(1993) by Martin Lynch, *Winners, Losers and Non-Runners* by Owen McCafferty (1992), *Justice* by Hugh Murphy (1992) and *Lengthening Shadows* by Graham Reid (1995).

Amateur Drama in Ulster

The on-going use of the Group Theatre as a home for amateur work testifies to the present health of the amateur drama movement in Ulster. From the efforts of the turn of the century dramatic societies to the Northern Drama League feises, and from the Ulster Group Theatre competitions to the current wealth of amateur drama festivals, this sector of the arts community has had the most consistent history of any throughout this century. Throughout the difficult years of the 1970s, when most of the professional theatres were forced to close, the amateur drama movement steadfastly continued to operate at community level. It has since maintained an admirable strength and geographical spread which testifies to the vital grass-roots popularity of drama in Ulster. As well as producing work for consideration in its own right, amateur drama has proved the seeding ground for many professional performers and companies in Ulster. Hence, to do justice to the amateur drama world would require an exhibition and guide singularly devoted to the movement itself. This is an area on which the archive hopes to concentrate in the future. Meanwhile, given the impossibility of any kind of comprehensive coverage, it would be invidious to select individual groups for reference.

Youth Theatre

Youth theatre is one of the best established areas of community arts provision throughout the province, and represents 'an interesting mix of statutory and private provision'.[267] As well as being attached to professional theatres such as the Lyric and the Arts, youth theatres can also be connected to amateur drama groups (Newpoint Players, Newry) or youth organisations (the Rainbow Factory at Youth Action). The longest-established youth drama provision was set up by the Arts Council of Northern Ireland in the late 1970s as the Youth Drama Scheme. This operated as a network of regional centres, and initially concentrated on process-oriented work under the directorship of Denis Smyth. A more performance-related approach then emerged, culminating in 1982 in the first Ulster Youth Theatre event, centred around a new play, *Ricochets* by Martin Lynch. Funding pressures subsequently resulted in the adoption of a more commercial approach, and a series of highly successful musicals were directed by Michael Poynor at the Grand Opera House, Belfast. In 1987, the focus of the UYT changed again with the appointment of Imelda Foley as Drama Development Officer of the Arts Council. Nick Philippou directed a series of productions, including Shakespeare and devised projects such as *Stations*. In 1992 David Grant became Artistic Director; productions since then have included *Goodnight Strabane* by Gerard Stembridge, *Brave New World* (1992), *Cyrano de Bergerac* (1994), *The Seven Deadly Sins* (1995), *Ghetto* (1996) and *Under Milk Wood* (1997). During this 15 year period, the regional centres have continued to operate, and to feed into the summer production. In the light of increasing diversity in this sector, with no less than four major summer productions in 1997 alone, for example, the whole support structure for youth drama is under review at the time of writing.

Community Drama

Since the pioneering days of Fr. Des Wilson's People's Theatre at Ballymurphy, and Martin Lynch's Turf Lodge Fellowship Community Theatre in the 1970s, the community drama sector has become one of the busiest in the entire theatre community. The growth, range, and sheer diversity of the activities undertaken to 1993 have been well charted by David Grant in the Community Relations Council publication, *Playing the Wild Card*. The movement has, however, developed considerably even since then. This recent process has been recorded by *The CAN*, the magazine of the Community Arts Forum (CAF). The creation of this umbrella body in 1993 testifies to the increasing strength of the community arts movement. Established partly for lobbying purposes, CAF's initial aims also included establishing a sense of solidarity and providing opportunities for the exchange of experiences and ideas. The initial twelve groups who founded the body have since been joined by almost one hundred others, 'incorporating every art form imaginable'.[268] The work of these, and other such companies, is resulting in an evident widening of the cultural franchise, a process still 'growing at a phenomenal rate'.[269] As with the amateur companies, achieving proper representation of the community arts is an archival priority for the future. Given the impossibility of proper coverage in the present context, the reader is referred to *The CAN* and to *Playing the Wild Card* for individual community theatre histories.

NOTES AND REFERENCES

The Eighteenth Century

[1] Address at opening of the new theatre in Rosemary Lane, Belfast, March 3, 1784. Quoted in Lawrence, W..J., *The Annals of the Old Belfast Stage*. Prepared for publication in 1896, but never actually published; copy held in archive.

[2] Adams. J.R.R., *The Printed Word and the Common Man, Popular Culture in Ulster 1700–1900*. Belfast: Institute of Irish Studies, the Queen's University of Belfast, p. 69.

[3] Greene, John C. and Gladys L.H. Clark, *The Dublin Stage*, 1720–1745. London and Toronto: Associated University Presses, 1993, p. 81.

[4] Clark, William Smith, *The Irish Stage in the County Towns, 1720–1880*. Oxford: Clarendon Press, 1965, pp. 1–2.

[5] Greene and Clark, *The Dublin Stage, 1720–1745*. p. 45.

[6] Curtis, George Tickner, *A Treatise on the Law of Copyright in Books, Dramatic and Musical Compositions, Letters and other Manuscripts, Engravings and Sculptures, as enacted and administered in England and America; with some notes of the history of literary property*. London: A. Maxwell and Son, 1847.

[7] Pollard, M, *Dublin's Trade in Books 1550–1800*. Lyell Lectures, 1986–1987. Oxford: Clarendon Press, 1989. p. 67.

[8] Clark, *The Irish Stage in the County Towns, 1720–1880*. p. 287.

[9] Ibid., p. 289.

[10] Ibid., p. 288.

[11] Bernard, John, *Retrospections of the Stage*. In two volumes. London: Henry Colburn and Richard Bentley. Vol. 1, p. 330.

[12] Ibid., p. 306.

[13] Greene and Clark, *The Dublin Stage, 1720–1745*. p. 51.

[14] Ibid., p. 39.

[15] Bernard, *Retrospections of the Stage*, p. 328.

[16] Clark, *The Irish Stage in the County Towns, 1720–1880*, p. 4.

[17] Greene and Clarke, *The Dublin Stage, 1720–1745*. p. 41.

[18] Ibid., p. 72.

[19] Clark, *The Irish Stage in the County Towns, 1720–1880*, p. 191.

[20] *Newry Commercial Telegraph,* November 24, 1818; quoted in Clarke, loc. cit., p. 195.

[21] *Belfast News-Letter*, October 1790, quoted in Lawrence, p. 148.

[22] Clark, *The Irish Stage in the County Towns, 1720–1880*, p. 200.

[23] *Londonderry Journal*, May 22, 1786. Quoted in Clarke, p. 206.

[24] Clark, *The Irish Stage in the County Towns, 1720–1880*, p. 206.

[25] Ibid., p. 207.

[26] Ibid., p. 251.

[27] Lawrence, *The Annals of the Old Belfast Stage*, p. 39.

[28] Ibid., p. 39.

[29] Ibid., p. 76.

[30] Bernard, *Retrospections of the Stage*, p. 323

[31] *Belfast News-Letter,* June 17, 1783.

[32] Ibid., June 20, 1783.

[33] *The Belfast Mercury,* March 5, 1784.

[34] Lawrence, *The Annals of the Old Belfast Stage*, p. 156.

[35] *Northern Star,* February 6, 1793. Quoted in Lawrence, p. 165.

[36] Bernard, *Retrospections of the Stage*, p. 369.

[37] *The Drennan Letters, being a selection of the correspondence which passed between William*

Drennan and his brother-in-law and sister Samuel and Martha McTier during the years 1776–1819. Ed. D.A. Chart. Belfast: H.M. Stationary Office, 1931. p. 138.

[38]Lawrence, *The Annals of the Old Belfast Stage,* p. 88.

[39]Clark, *The Irish Stage in the County Towns, 1720–1880,* pp. 252–3.

[40]Lawrence, *The Annals of the Old Belfast Stage,* p. 79.

[41]Ibid., p. 87.

[42]Ibid., p. 88.

[43]Clark, *The Irish Stage in the County Towns, 1720–1880,* p. 252.

[44]Lawrence, *The Annals of the Old Belfast Stage,* p. 129.

[45]Bermard, *Retrospections of the Stage,* p. 363.

[46]Clark, *The Irish Stage in the County Towns, 1720–1880,* p. 274.

[47]Ibid., p. 275.

[48]*Belfast News-Letter,* October 6, 1794.

[49]*The Drennan Letters,* p. 281.

[50]Clark, *The Irish Stage in the County Towns, 1720–1880,* p. 214.

[51]Ibid.

[52]*Belfast News-Letter,* December 6, 1799, quoted in Clark, p. 282.

The Nineteenth Century

[1]Appeal to the press by Thomas Drew, quoted in Hempton, David and Myrtle Hill, *Evangelical Protestantism in Ulster Society, 1740–1890.* London: Routledge, 1992, p. 117.

[2]Bardon, Jonathan, *A History of Ulster.* Belfast: Blackstaff Press, p. 243.

[3]*The Drennan Letters,* McTier, ref. 837, p. 299.

[4]Ibid., McTier, ref. 1136, p. 341.

[5]Ibid., McTier, ref. 1175, p. 349.

[6]Ibid., McTier, ref. 1225, p. 355.

[7]Ibid., McTier, ref. 1125, pp. 338–9.

[8]*Belfast News-Letter,* April 30, 1805. Quoted in Lawrence, p. 257.

[9]*Belfast News-Letter,* February 14, 1804. Ibid., p. 257.

[10]*Belfast News-Letter,* November 1806. Ibid., p. 298.

[11]Lawrence, *The Annals of the Old Belfast Stage,* p. 407.

[12]*The Northern Whig,* October 6, 1842.

[13]*Belfast News-Letter,* December 5, 1820.

[14]Lawrence, *The Annals of the Old Belfast Stage,* p. 445.

[15]*The Northern Whig,* December 15, 1842.

[16]Ibid., September 24, 1842.

[17]Ibid., December 17, 1842.

[18]Ibid.

[19]Ibid.

[20]Booth, Michael. *Prefaces to English Nineteenth-Century Theatre.* Manchester: Manchester University Press, pp. 4–5.

[21]Booth, Michael, 'The Theatre and its Audience', in *The Revels History of Drama in English,* vol.VI, 1750–1880, gen. eds. Clifford Leech and T.W. Craik. London: Methuen and Company, p. 11.

[22]Bardon, Jonathan. *Belfast, an Illustrated History.* Belfast: Blackstaff Press, p. 66.

[23]Bardon, *Belfast, an Illustrated History,* p. 66.

[24]Lawrence, *The Annals of the Old Belfast Stage,* p. 290.

[25]Ibid., p. 373.

[26]Ibid., p. 431.

[27]Bardon, *Belfast, an Illustrated History,* p. 68.

[28]Booth, *Theatre and its Audience,* p. 21.

[29]*Belfast News-Letter,* December 5, 1820.

[30]Ibid.

[31]Harrison, J.F.C., *Early Victorian Britain, 1832–52.* London: Fontana Press, 1988, p. 133.

[32]Hempton, David and Myrtle Hill, *Evangelical Protestantism in Ulster Society, 1740–1890,* p. 113.

[33]*Lectures and Conversations, expressive of character and sentiment &c. &c.* Anonymous. Belfast: William Ferguson, 1837. pp. 28–29.

[34]Gray, John, 'Popular Entertainment', in *Belfast, the Making of a City,* J.C. Beckett *et al.* Belfast: Appletree Press, p. 107.

[35]Hempton and Hill, *Evangelical Protestantism in Ulster Society, 1740–1890,* p. 117.

[36]Thackeray, *The Irish Sketch Book,* p. 307.

[37]Hempton and Hill, *Evangelical Protestantism in Ulster Society, 1740–1890,* p. 119.

[38]Booth, Michael, *Prefaces to English Nineteenth-Century Theatre.* Manchester: Manchester University Press, p. 25.

[39]Thackeray, *The Irish Sketch Book,* p. 307.

[40]Booth, Michael, *The Theatre and its Audience,* p. 14.

[41]Ibid., p. 14.

[42]Ibid., p. 17.

[43]Ibid., p. 19.

[44]Booth, Michael, *Prefaces to English Nineteenth-Century Theatre.* p. 34.

[45]Ibid., p. 41.

[46]Ibid., p. 33.

[47]Bardon, *Belfast, an Illustrated History,* p. 89.

[48]Booth, Michael, *Prefaces to English Nineteenth-Century Theatre,* p. 20.

[49]*The Magpie,* March 24, 1900.

[50]*Belfast News-Letter,* September 28, 1882.

[51]*The Tatler,* No. 37, March 12, 1902.

[52]*Nomad's Weekly,* March 1, 1902.

[53]Ibid., July 5, 1902.

[54]Gray, John, *Popular Entertainment,* p. 109.

[55]*The Morning News and Examiner,* Belfast, April 8, 1886.

[56]*Belfast News-Letter,* December 17, 1895. Quoted in *Frank Matcham, Theatre Architect,* ed. Brian Mercer Walker. Belfast: Blackstaff Press, 1980, p. 97.

[57]*Belfast News-Letter,* December 17, 1895, quoted in Matcham, Brian Walker, p. 96.

[58]*Northern Whig,* December 1, 1895, quoted in Matcham, Brian Walker, p. 95.

[59]*Belfast News-Letter,* December 17, 1895, quoted in Matcham, Brian Walker, p. 95.

[60]*The Magpie,* February 18, 1899.

[61]*Northern Whig,* August 21, 1901.

[62]Ibid.

[63]Ibid., August 20, 1901.

[64]*Ireland's Saturday Night,* October 19, 1901.

[65]*Evening Telegraph,* February 5, 1901.

[66]*Ireland's Saturday Night,* January 4, 1902.

[67]Anonymous letter to *Ireland's Saturday Night,* January 14, 1899.

[68]*The Official Report of the Church [of Ireland] Conference,* held at Armagh, September, 1892. Belfast: Olley & Co., p. 21.

[69]Letter from Fred W. Warden to the Editor of the *Belfast News-Letter,* April 25, 1901.

[70]*Ireland's Saturday Night,* October 19, 1901.

[71]Bardon, *Belfast, an Illustrated History,* p. 156.
[72]The Playgoer, in *The Belfast Critic,* November 10, 1900.

The Late Victorian and Edwardian Period

[1]*Belfast News-Letter,* January 17, 1900. Report of the Belfast Board of Guardians.
[2]Patton, Marcus, *Central Belfast, a Historical Gazetteer.* Belfast: Ulster Architectural Heritage Society, 1993, p. 18.
[3]*Belfast News-Letter,* June 9, 1881.
[4]Patton, Marcus, *Central Belfast, a Historical Gazetteer,* p. 18.
[5]*The Irish Builder,* October 15, 1871, pp. 262–263.
[6]*Belfast News-Letter,* June 9, 1881.
[7]Ibid.
[8]*Belfast News-Letter,* December 23, 1881.
[9]Gray, John, *Popular Entertainment,* p. 107.
[10]Gallagher, Lyn, *The Grand Opera House, Belfast.* Belfast: Blackstaff Press, 1995. p. 32.
[11]*Nomad's Weekly,* August 29, 1903.
[12]Ibid., January 30, 1904.
[13]Gallagher, Lyn, *The Grand Opera House,* Belfast, p. 38.
[14]*Belfast News-Letter,* March 11, 1915.
[15]Ibid.
[16]Open, Michael, *Fading Lights, Silver Screens, a History of Belfast Cinemas.* Antrim: Greystone Books, p. 73.
[17]Walker, Brian Mercer, *Frank Matcham, Theatre Architect.* Belfast: Blackstaff Press, 1980. p. 99.
[18]Gray, John, *Popular Entertainment,* p. 105.
[19]*Belfast News-Letter,* December 3, 1894.
[20]Ibid., December 3, 1894.
[21]Ibid., February 22, 1898.
[22]Ibid., January 25, 1898.
[23]Ibid., February 22, 1898.
[24]*Northern Whig,* February 4, 1955.
[25]*Nomad's Weekly,* June 21, 1902.
[26]Ibid., March 8, 1902.
[27]Bardon, *Belfast, an Illustrated History,* p. 223.
[28]*The Irish Independent,* October 12, 1932.
[29]*The Irish Times,* March 7, 1933.
[30]*Belfast Telegraph,* March 21, 1932.
[31]*Belfast News-Letter,* November 11, 1932.
[32]Gray, John (ed.), *Thomas Carnduff, Life and Writings.* Belfast: Lagan Press/ Fortnight Educational Trust, p. 29.
[33]*Irish News,* November 22, 1932.
[34]*Northern Whig,* November 22, 1932.
[35]*Belfast News-Letter,* November 22, 1932.
[36]Programme for *Workers* by Thomas Carnduff, presented by the Belfast Repertory Company at the Abbey Theatre, Dublin, October 10, 1932.
[37]*Belfast Telegraph,* November 22, 1932.
[38]*Irish News,* March 14, 1960.
[39]Ibid., March 14, 1960.
[40]*Northern Whig,* February 4, 1955.
[41]Patton, Marcus, *Central Belfast, a Historical Gazetteer,* p. 164.

[42]Gallagher, Lyn, *The Grand Opera House, Belfast*, p. 76.

[43]Ibid., p. 80.

[44]Open, Michael, *Fading Lights, Silver Screens*, p. 43.

[45]McKinstry, Robert, 'The Grand Opera House Belfast: restoring a Matcham theatre for today's audience and actors', in Walker, Brian Mercer, (ed.). *Frank Matcham, Theatre Architect*. Belfast: Blackstaff Press, 1980. p. 101.

[46]Patton, Marcus, *Central Belfast*, p. 164.

[47]*Annual Report of the Arts Council of Northern Ireland*, 1979/80, p. 17.

[48]Gallagher, Lyn, *Grand Opera House, Belfast*, p. 101.

[49]Ibid., p. 122.

[50]Ibid., p. 124.

[51]Patton, Marcus, *Central Belfast*, p. 164.

[52]*Belfast News-Letter*, April 2, 1907, p. 5.

[53]Open, Michael, *Fading Lights, Silver Screens*, p. 46.

[54]*Belfast News-Letter*, April 2, 1907, p. 5.

[55]Open, Michael, *Fading Lights, Silver Screens*, p. 46.

[56]Bardon, *Belfast, an Illustrated History*, p. 222.

[57]*Belfast Telegraph*, July 20, 1931.

[58]Ibid., January 4, 1939.

[59]*Ireland's Saturday Night*, May 23, 1942.

[60]*Belfast Telegraph*, April 10, 1961.

[61]Ibid., September 28, 1961.

[62]*Belfast News-Letter*, October 14, 1961.

[63]Open, Michael, *Fading Lights, Silver Screens*, p. 46.

[64]Patton, Marcus, *Central Belfast*, p. 164.

The Twentieth Century

[1]Editorial note, first edition of *Uladh*, Samhain number, November 1904.

[2]Editorial note, second edition of *Uladh*, Feil Brighde number, Feb. 1905.

[3]Bell, Sam Hanna, *The Theatre in Ulster*, Dublin: Gill and Macmillan Ltd., 1972.

[4]Mayne, Rutherford, 'The Ulster Literary Theatre', *The Dublin Magazine*, vol. 31 (1955), pp. 15–21.

[5]Mengel, Hagal, *Sam Thompson and Modern Drama in Ulster*, Frankfurt am Main: Verlag Peter Lang, 1986.

[6]Mengel, *Sam Thompson and Modern Drama in Ulster*, p. 23.

[7]Letter from Bulmer Hobson to Sam Hanna Bell. Quoted in Bell, Sam Hanna, *The Theatre in Ulster*, p. 2.

[8]Ibid.

[9]Ibid.

[10]Ibid., p. 4.

[11]Editorial note, first edition of *Uladh*, Samhain number, November 1904.

[12]Bell, *The Theatre in Ulster*, p. 16.

[13]Ibid., p. 38.

[14]Mengel, Hagal, *Sam Thompson and Modern Drama in Ulster*, p. 46.

[15]Maxwell, D.E.S., *A Critical History of Modern Irish Drama, 1891–1980*. Cambridge: Cambridge University Press, p. 65.

[16]Mengel, *Sam Thompson and Modern Drama in Ulster*, p. 43.

[17]Ibid., p. 41.

[18]Killen, John, Introduction to *Rutherford Mayne, Selected Plays*. Belfast: Institute of Irish Studies, 1997.

[19]McHenry, Margaret, *The Ulster Theatre in Ireland*. University of Pennsylvania, 1931, p. 64.

[20]Mengel, *Sam Thompson and Modern Drama in Ulster*, p. 73.

[21]Hogan, Robert, ed.-in-chief, *Dictionary of Irish Literature*. London: Aldwych Press, p. 837.

[22]Reid, Forrest, 'Eighteen Years Work', in *The Times*, supplement, December 5, 1922. Quoted by Mengel, op. cit., p. 108.

[23]Hogan, Robert and Michael J. O'Neill, eds. *Joseph Holloway's Abbey Theatre*. Southern Illinois University Press, 1967.

[24]*Samhain*, November, 1908.

[25]Bell, *The Theatre in Ulster*, p. 49.

[26]Reid, Forrest, 'Eighteen Years Work'. Quoted by Mengel, loc. cit., p. 161.

[27]Quoted in Bell, *The Theatre in Ulster*, p. 49.

[28]Bell, *The Theatre in Ulster*, p. 49.

[29]Mengel, *Sam Thompson and Modern Drama in Ulster*, p. 43.

[30]Kane, Whitford, *Are We All Met?* London: Elkin Mathews and Marrot, 1931, p. 108.

[31]Mengel, *Sam Thompson and Modern Drama in Ulster*, p. 108.

[32]Bell, *The Theatre in Ulster*, p. 49.

[33]Mengel, *Sam Thompson and Modern Drama in Ulster*, p. 112.

[34]Bell, *The Theatre in Ulster*, p. 51.

[35]Kennedy, David, 'The Drama in Ulster', in *The Arts in Ulster*, ed. Sam Hanna Bell, Nesca A. Robb, John Hewitt. London: George G. Harrap, 1951, p. 57.

[36]Quoted by Mengel, *Sam Thompson and Modern Drama in Ulster*, p. 112.

[37]Northern Drama League circular, held in archive, dated 1923.

[38]'Doll's House' in Belfast', *Belfast Telegraph*, January 19, 1929.

[39]Kennedy, David, *The Drama in Ulster*, loc. cit., p. 66.

[40]*Belfast Telegraph*, January 21, 1933.

[41]*Belfast News-Letter*, February 10, 1933.

[42]*Belfast Telegraph*, January 24, 1933.

[43]*Belfast News-Letter*, July 6, 1933.

[44]'The Plays Preferred', in *The Little Theatre, Belfast*, a brochure held at the National Library, Dublin, n.d.

[45]*Belfast Telegraph*, December 15, 1936.

[46]*Belfast News-Letter*, April 20, 1937.

[47]*Belfast News-Letter*, April 27, 1937.

[48]Ibid., April 20, 1937.

[49]Ibid., February 14, 1939, p. 7.

[50]Kennedy, David. *The Drama in Ulster*, p. 58.

[51]Shiels' letter held in archive, dated May 13, 1940.

[52]Shiels' letter held in archive, dated February 6, 1941.

[53]Shiels' letter held in archive, dated November 28, 1946.

[54]*Belfast News-Letter*, August 24, 1960.

[55]*Belfast Telegraph*, December 17, 1958.

[56]Ibid., May 7, 1958.

[57]Memorandum and Articles of Association for the Ulster Group Theatre Limited, incorporated the 23rd day of May, 1958, held in archive.

[58]'Guarantees against Loss for Group and Arts Theatres', *Belfast Telegraph*, November 4, 1958.

[59]*Belfast Telegraph*, December 18, 1958.

[60]Ibid., December 17, 1958.

[61] Ibid., May 7, 1959.

[62] Mengel, Hagal, *Sam Thompson and Modern Drama in Ulster.* Frankfurt am Main, P. Lang, 1986, p. 304.

[63] *Belfast Telegraph,* May 13, 1959.

[64] *Belfast News-Letter,* September 9, 1958.

[65] Ibid., September 2, 1958.

[66] Ibid.

[67] *Belfast Telegraph,* May 19, 1959.

[68] Ibid., May 12, 1959.

[69] Ibid., May 10, 1959.

[70] Ibid., May 2, 1959.

[71] Ibid., October 23, 1959.

[72] Ibid.

[73] Ibid., November 5, 1959.

[74] Knipe, John, 'The James Young Era', in *The Group Theatre, a Souvenir History.* Belfast: Group Theatre, n.d., p. 16.

[75] Bardon, Jonathan, *Belfast, an Illustrated History,* p. 257.

[76] *Belfast Telegraph,* January 20, 1960.

[77] Ibid., September 29, 1960.

[78] Ibid., September 14, 1960.

[79] Ibid.

[80] Knipe, John, 'The James Young Era', pp. 16–17.

[81] *Belfast Telegraph,* July 7, 1961.

[82] Ibid., May 15, 1961.

[83] Ibid., June 4, 1964.

[84] Ibid., July 6, 1974.

[85] Ibid., November 2, 1973.

[86] Bardon, Jonathan, *Belfast, an Illustrated History,* p. 311.

[87] Ibid., p. 309.

[88] Leaflet in archive, 'Welcome Back to the Group Theatre', not dated.

[89] *Belfast Telegraph,* October 16, 1971.

[90] *Northern Whig,* February 11, 1947.

[91] Bell, Sam Hanna, *The Theatre in Ulster.* Dublin: Gill and Macmillan, 1972, p. 108.

[92] *Northern Whig,* February 11, 1947.

[93] Wilmot, Hubert R, 'The Belfast Arts Theatre'. In *The Stage in Ulster,* brochure for Carter's Series of Irish Plays. Belfast: H.R. Carter Publications, [1950], p.7.

[94] Wilmot, Hubert R, The 'Belfast Arts Theatre'. In *The Stage in Ulster,* brochure for Carter's Series of Irish Plays. Belfast: H.R. Carter Publications, [1950], p.8.

[95] *Northern Whig,* February 11, 1947.

[96] Wilmot, Hubert R, 'The Belfast Arts Theatre'. In *The Stage in Ulster,* brochure for Carter's Series of Irish Plays. Belfast: H.R. Carter Publications, [1950], p. 9.

[97] *Belfast Telegraph,* September 9, 1948.

[98] *Northern Whig,* April 24, 1947.

[99] *Belfast Telegraph,* March 25, 1948.

[100] The new name, dropping 'Studio' from the title, had evidently been tried earlier. A laminated poster in the archive describes the company as The Arts Theatre at North Street.

[101] Bell, *The Theatre in Ulster,* p. 109.

[102] Ibid., p. 109.

[103] *Belfast Telegraph,* January 2, 1961.

[104] *I.S.N.,* April 2, 1949.

[105] *Belfast Telegraph,* January 21, 1951.

[106] *Belfast News-Letter,* September 5, 1952.

[107] *Arts Council of Northern Ireland Annual Report, 1970/71,* p. 13.

[108] Fitz-Simon, Christopher, *The Irish Theatre.* London: Thames and Hudson, 1983, p. 193.

[109] *Belfast Telegraph,* March 21, 1961

[110] Ibid., April 17, 1961

[111] Ibid., April 18, 1961.

[112] Ibid., June 24, 1961

[113] Ibid., February 6, 1962

[114] *Belfast Telegraph,* February 3, 1962

[115] *Belfast News-Letter,* August 27, 1962

[116] *Belfast Telegraph,* April 17, 1964

[117] *Arts Council of Northern Ireland Annual Report,* 1970–71, p. 15.

[118] *Belfast Telegraph,* August 15, 1970.

[119] *Arts Council of Northern Ireland Annual Report,* 1970–71, p. 15.

[120] Ibid., p. 13

[121] *Arts Council of Northern Ireland Annual Report, 1969–70,* p. 18.

[122] *Arts Council of Northern Ireland Annual Report, 1970–71,* p. 15.

[123] *Arts Council of Northern Ireland Annual Report, 1969–70,* p. 20.

[124] *Belfast Telegraph,* August 15, 1970.

[125] Ibid., August 15, 1970.

[126] Ibid., August 20, 1970.

[127] Ibid., January 15, 1971.

[128] Ibid., October 16, 1971

[129] *Belfast News-Letter,* October 14, 1971

[130] *Arts Council of Northern Ireland Annual Report* 1972/3, p. 17.

[131] *Belfast Telegraph,* October 27, 1973.

[132] Ibid., November 16, 1976.

[133] Ibid.

[134] *Arts Council of Northern Ireland Annual Report,* 1977/8, p. 23.

[135] *Arts Council of Northern Ireland Annual Report,* 1979/80, p. 8.

[136] *Arts Council of Northern Ireland Annual Report,* 1980/81, p.6.

[137] *Belfast Telegraph,* November 16, 1976.

[138] Ibid., August 13, 1983.

[139] *Arts Council of Northern Ireland Annual Report,* 1984/5, p. 10.

[140] Belfast Civic Arts Theatre Refurbishment Appeal Fund brochure, February 1986, held in archive.

[141] Radio script in archive, 'Lyric Players Theatre', for *The Arts in Ulster* series, broadcast Northern Ireland Home Service, February 10, 1966.

[142] Ibid.

[143] *The Artist and the Theatre,* lecture to Belfast Society of Women Artists by Mary O'Malley. Appendix D in *A Poet's Theatre* by Conor O'Malley, Dublin: Elo Press, 1988.

[144] Ibid.

[145] Actor Frances McShane quoted from radio script in archive, 'Lyric Players Theatre', for *The Arts in Ulster* series.

[146] O'Malley, Mary. *Never Shake Hands With the Devil.* Dublin: Elo Publications, 1990, p. 57.

[147] O'Malley, Mary, *Never Shake Hands...,* p. 57

[148] Brochure in archive, *The Lyric Theatre, 1951–1968.* Belfast: Lyric Players Theatre, 1968.

[149]Rosenfield, Ray, 'It All Started Like This...', in *The Lyric Players Belfast, 1951–68*. Belfast: Lyric Players Theatre, 1968.

[150]O'Malley, *Never Shake Hands,* p. 70.

[151]Rosenfield, Ray, 'It All Started Like This...'.

[152]Boyle, J.W., 'The First Five Years', in *The Lyric Players, Belfast, 1951–1956*. Belfast: Lyric Players Theatre, 1956.

[153]Boyle, J.W., 'The Making of a Theatre 1951–68', in *A Needle's Eye,* Belfast: Lyric Players Theatre, 1979.

[154]O'Malley, Mary, *Never Shake Hands...,* p. 89.

[155]Ibid., p. 95.

[156]Actor Joan McCready quoted from radio script in archive, 'Lyric Players Theatre', for *The Arts in Ulster* series.

[157]Ibid.

[158]Lyric Players Theatre Trust, *Deed of Declaration of Trust,* dated May 3, 1960, held in archive.

[159]O'Malley, Mary, *Never Shake Hands...,* p. 171.

[160]O'Malley, Conor, *A Poet's Theatre.* Dublin: Elo Publications, p. 28.

[161]Ibid., p. 28.

[162]*The Irish Times,* June 10, 1965.

[163]O'Malley, Mary, *Never Shake Hands...,* p. 221.

[164]*Belfast News-Letter,* November 22, 1969.

[165]O'Malley, Mary, *Never Shake Hands...,* p. 215.

[166]Copy of letter in archive dated March 24, 1969, from the Lyric Players Theatre Trustees and addressed to 'Dear Member and Subscriber'.

[167]*Belfast News-Letter,* November 22, 1969.

[168]*The Irish Times,* November 8, 1969.

[169]*Belfast News-Letter,* November 22, 1969.

[170]*Belfast Telegraph,* December 16, 1969.

[171]*Annual Report of the Arts Council of Northern Ireland,* 1969/70, p. 18.

[172]O'Malley, Mary, *Never Shake Hands...,* p. 307.

[173]*Annual Report of the Arts Council of Northern Ireland,* 1969/70, p. 18.

[174]O'Malley, Mary, *Never Shake Hands...,* p. 256.

[175]Ibid., p. 311.

[176]*Belfast Telegraph,* June 29, 1973.

[177]O'Malley, Conor, *A Poet's Theatre,* p. 36.

[178]McKeown, Ciaran, 'Can Belfast Live With a Poets' Theatre?' In *A Needle's Eye,* p. 76.

[179]*Annual Report of the Arts Council of Northern Ireland,* 1989, p. 28.

[180]O'Malley, Conor, *A Poet's Theatre,* p. 125/6.

[181]*Annual Report of the Arts Council of Northern Ireland,* 1983/4, p. 10.

[182]*Annual Report of the Arts Council of Northern Ireland,* 1986/7, p. 20.

[183]*Annual Report of the Arts Council of Northern Ireland,* 1991, p. 31.

[184]Ibid., p. 29.

[185]*Annual Report of the Arts Council of Northern Ireland,* 1993/4, p. 13.

[186]*Belfast Telegraph,* October 14, 1965.

[187]*Annual Report of the Arts Council of Northern Ireland,* 1967/8, p. 12.

[188]*Belfast Telegraph,* October 1, 1965.

[189]O'Malley, Mary, *Never Shake Hands...,* p. 190.

[190]Ibid., p. 190.

[191]Ibid., p. 191.

[192]*Belfast Telegraph,* November 2, 1965.

[193]*Belfast News-Letter,* January 6, 1966.

[194]*Belfast Telegraph,* January 1, 1966.

[195]*Belfast News-Letter,* September 29, 1966.

[196]Ibid..

[197]*Annual Report of Arts Council of Northern Ireland,* 1967/8, p. 13.

[198]Ibid., pp. 12–13.

[199]*Annual Report of Arts Council of Northern Ireland,* 1969/70, p. 18.

[200]Ibid.

[201]*Belfast Telegraph,* September 3, 1971.

[202]Mary Holland, 'Field Day's Tenth Birthday', in programme for *The Cure at Troy,* 1990.

[203]'Field Day Theatre Co. to Present Chekhov's *Three Sisters*', *Derry Journal,* 19 June 1985, p. 5. Quoted in Marilynn J. Richtarik, *Acting Between the Lines, The Field Day Theatre Company and Irish Cultural Politics 1980–1984.* Oxford: Clarendon Press, 1994, p. 109.

[204]*Annual Report of the Arts Council of Northern Ireland,* 1989, p. 28.

[205]Richtarick, *Acting Between the Lines,* p. 237

[206]'Preface', *Ireland's Field Day: Field Day Theatre Company,* London: Hutchinson and Co., 1985, vii. Quoted in Anthony Roche's *Contemporary Irish Drama,* p. 243.

[207]Boland, Eavan, 'Poets and Pamphlets', *Irish Times,* October 1, 1983. Quoted in Richtarik, Marilynn J., *Acting Between the Lines,* p. 159.

[208]Mary Holland, 'Field Day's Tenth Birthday', in programme for *The Cure at Troy,* 1990.

[209]Richtarik, Marilynn J., *Acting Between the Lines,* p. 238.

[210]Hadfield, Paul, 'Field Day, Over But Not Out', in *Theatre Ireland* 31, p. 47.

[211]Ibid., p. 47.

[212]Ibid., p. 48.

[213]Richtarik, Marilynn J., *Acting Between the Lines,* p. 3.

[214]Roche, Anthony. *Contemporary Irish Drama from Beckett to McGuinness.* Dublin: Gill and Macmillan, 1994, p. 244.

[215]O'Toole, Fintan. 'Unsung Heroines Take a Bow', in *The Irish Times,* June 2, 1990.

[216]Eleanor Methven, quoted in 'Staging a Little Irish History', *The Boston Globe,* February 14, 1986.

[217]Janet Mackle, quoted by Jane Coyle, 'Charabanc in Top Gear', *The Irish News,* August 10, 1984.

[218]Marie Jones, from the draft copy of an interview with Charabanc by Carol Martin for publication in *The Drama Review.* Copy dated November 8, 1986, and held in the archive.

[219]Carol Scanlan, ibid.

[220]Eleanor Methven, ibid.

[221]Article by Helen Lojak in archive, *Playing Politics: Northern Ireland, Women, Theatre and Charabanc.*

[222]*Time Out, London's Weekly Guide,* November 15–21, 1984.

[223]Jane Coyle, 'Charabanc in Top Gear', *The Irish News,* August 10, 1984.

[224]DiCenzo, Maria R. 'Charabanc Theatre Company: Placing Women Centre-Stage in Northern Ireland', in *Theatre Journal* 45, (1993), John Hopkins University Press.

[225]JS, 'Piercing, Patient Observation', *Fortnight,* November 1986.

[226]*The Irish Times,* December 29, 1987.

[227]Ibid., March 31, 1987.

[228]*Time Out, London's Weekly Guide,* November 15–21, 1984.

[229]DiCenzo, Maria R, 'Charabanc Theatre Company: Placing Women Centre-Stage in Northern Ireland'.

[230]Harris, Claudia, 'Somewhere Over the Balcony at the Drill Hall' in *Theatre Ireland,* November 1987.

[231]Interview with Jane Coyle, 'Stage Tribute to Women of Divis', *The Irish News,* May 31, 1988.

[232]DiCenzo, Maria R. *Charabanc Theatre Company: Placing Women Centre-Stage in Northern Ireland,* p. 37.

[233]Ibid.

[234]Letter in archive from Maureen Jordan, Chairperson for Charabanc Theatre Company's Board of Directors to Lynda Henderson, Editor, *Theatre Ireland,* dated November 6, 1990.

[235]Edwardes, Jane, in *Time Out, London's Weekly Guide,* May 9–16, 1990.

[236]*Belfast News-Letter,* February 2, 1990.

[237]*Stage and Television Today,* March 22, 1990.

[238]Brighton, Pam, 'Charabanc', *Theatre Ireland* (23), pp. 41–42.

[239]Letter in archive from Maureen Jordan, Chairperson for Charabanc Theatre Company's Board of Directors to Lynda Henderson, Editor, *Theatre Ireland,* dated November 6, 1990.

[240]DiCenzo, Maria R. 'Charabanc Theatre Company: Placing Women Centre-Stage in Northern Ireland', p. 37.

[241]Charabanc Theatre Company Mission Statement, 1995, held in archive.

[242]Hill, Ian, review of *Me and My Friend* in *The Guardian,* February 14, 1991.

[243]Review of *Bondagers* in *The Guardian,* October 24, 1991.

[244]Review of *Skirmishes* in *The Irish Times,* November 20, 1992.

[245]Lojek, Helen, 'Seeking New Writing, Seeking More Analysis', in *Irish Studies Review,* No. 8, Autumn 1994, p. 30.

[246]Rosenfield, Ray, *The Irish Times,* August 8, 1991.

[247]Hill, Ian, *The Guardian,* August 9, 1991.

[248]*The Irish Times,* April 14, 1992.

[249]*Sunday Life,* May 3, 1992.

[250]*The Independent,* October 28, 1994.

[251]*The Irish Times,* February 25, 1995.

[252]*Belfast Telegraph,* February 28, 1995.

[253]*The Sunday Times,* March 12, 1995.

[254]Charabanc press release held in archive, dated July 10, 1995.

[255]DiCenzo, Maria R. 'Charabanc Theatre Company: Placing Women Centre-Stage in Northern Ireland' in *Theatre Journal* 45 (1993), John Hopkins University Press, p. 38.

[256]Ibid.

[257]Programme, *A Night in November* by Marie Jones, DubbelJoint Productions 1993.

[258]*Belfast Telegraph,* August 9, 1994.

[259]Programme, *Stones in his Pockets* by Marie Jones, DubbelJoint Productions 1996.

[260]*Arts Council of Northern Ireland Annual Report,* 1995/6, p. 22.

[261]O Muiri, Pol, 'One-sided view of the struggle in West Belfast', *The Irish Times,* August 12, 1997.

[262]Brighton, Pam, 'Drama's Portrayal of Forgotten Injustices', *The Irish News,* August 14, 1997.

[263]*Arts Council of Northern Ireland Annual Report,* 1995/6, p. 22.

[264]*Arts Council of Northern Ireland Annual Report,* 1993, p. 30.

[265]Ibid., p. 30.

[266]*Arts Council of Northern Ireland Annual Report,* 1995/6, p. 22

[267] Grant, David, *Playing the Wild Card, Community Drama and Smaller-scale Professional Theatre*. Belfast: Community Relations Council, 1993, p. 52.
[268] *The CAN,* Issue 4, Winter 1996. Belfast: Community Arts Forum, p. 2.
[269] *The CAN,* Issue 4, Winter 1996. Belfast: Community Arts Forum, p. 2.

Illustrations

1. Mr. Kean as Richard III. Not dated, published by J. Lodge, Dawson Street.
2. Burnham as Claude Melmotte in *The Lady of Lyons*. Presented by J.F.Warden's stock company at the Theatre Royal, Belfast, 1871. Photograph: D.Welch.
3. Mr. Forbes-Robertson in *The Passing of the Third Floor Back* by Jerome K. Jerome. From an undated commemorative booklet on the production held in the archive, photograph by Messrs. Foulsham and Banfield, London. Forbes-Robertson appeared at the Grand Opera House, Belfast, in November 1900.
4. Charabanc Theatre Company Irish première of *Bondagers* by Sue Glover, staged autumn 1991. Photograph: Jill Jennings. Left to right: Lynn Cahill, Michèle Forbes and Paula McFetridge. Reproduced by kind permission of the company.
5. One of the Ulster Group Theatre productions of *Right Again Barnum* by Joseph Tomelty. Left to right: John McDaid, Jack O'Malley.

Exhibition Catalogue

John McDaid and Jack O'Malley in an Ulster Group Theatre production of *Right Again Barnum* by Joseph Tomelty.

The Eighteenth and Nineteenth Centuries
Illustrations
1. Poster of the Theatre, Newry, October 26. 1807. *Percy, Earl of Northumberland,* and *Ducks and Peas, or the New-Castle Epicure.*.
2. Sketch of Edmund Keane as Richard the III, n.d., pub. J. Lodge, Dawson Street. Handbill for the historical tragedy, *Brutus,* featuring Edmund Kean, at the Belfast Theatre on November 22, 1824.
3. Poster, 'Theatre Royal', Hillsborough. Private theatricals under the patronage of the Marchioness of Downshire featuring the comic opera, *No Song, No Supper.* Not dated, midnineteenth century.
4. Silk poster. 'Theatre Royal', Clandeboye. Private theatricals, featuring *The Fallen Pear, or Harlequin in Paris,* January 1849.

Case Items
5. Hitchcock. Robert. *An Historical View of the Irish Stage from the Earliest Period to the Close of the Season 1778.* Vol. 1. Dublin: R. Marchbank, 1788.
6. Michelburne, John (attrib.) *Ireland Preserved, or the Siege of Londonderry.* Belfast: Smyth, High Street, 1830.
7. Ashton, Robert. *The Battle of Aughrim, or, the Fall of Monsieur St. Ruth, a tragedy.* Belfast: Smyth and Lyons, 1808.
8. Goldsmith, Oliver. *She Stoops to Conquer, or the Mistakes of a Night.* Belfast: James Magee, 1773.
9. Stevens, George Alexander. (attrib.) *The Trip to Portsmouth.* James Magee, 1774.
10. Kelly, Hugh. *Clementina, a tragedy.* Belfast: Henry and Robert Joy, 1771.
11. O'Keeffe, John. *The Poor Soldier, a comic opera.* Belfast: James Magee, 1785.
12. Bernard, John. *Retrospections of the Stage.* Vol. 1. London: Henry Colburn and Richard Bentley, 1830.
13. *The Drennan Letters. Being a selection from the correspondence which passed between William Drennan, M.D., and his brother-in-law and sister Samuel and Martha McTier during the years 1776–1819.* Belfast: His Majesty's Stationery Office, 1931.
14. *The Lectures and Conversations Expressive of Character and Sentiment.* Anonymous. Belfast: William Ferguson, 1837.
15. *The Parliamentary Gazeteer of Ireland, 1843–1844.* Dublin, London and Edinburgh: A. Fullerton and Company, 1844.
16. Drawing of Fred Warden, theatre manager. In *The Magpie,* April 22, 1899.

Late Victorian and Early Twentieth Century
Illustrations
17. Photographs of actors from the stock company of the Theatre Royal, Belfast, 1871. Top: Burnham as Claude Melmotte in *The Lady of Lyons.* Bottom: Adams as Wanatee the Indian in *The Octaroon.*
18. Poster, Theatre Royal, January 12, 1914. The Belfast Dramatic Society in *The Bells,* by M.M. Erchmann-Chatrian, preceded by *Ich on Parle Francais,* a farce by Thomas J. Williams.
19. Handbills of productions at the Grand Opera House, Belfast. All undated, but *The Desert Song* was first produced at Drury Lane on April 7, 1927. *The Girl in the Taxi* was produced at the Lyric Theatre in 1912. Phyllis Dare (postcard) featured as Yvette in *The Street Singer,* which this publicises, in 1924. There are no dates available for *The Girl on the Film. Lilac Time* was first played in 1922 at the Lyric, London, and revived at Daly's Theatre in 1927 and 1928.

Case Items

20. Wages and Accounts Book for the Theatre Royal, Belfast. dated 1871–1901, and Reports and Accounts for the period from 31 January 1915 to February 5, 1916.

21. Four programmes from the Theatre Royal. Belfast. 1) Handbill for Carl Rosa Opera Company Belfast season. August 1884. 2) Front detail of programmes for Theatre Royal, early 1890s. 3) Front detail of Theatre Royal programmes, late 1890s. 4) F.R. Benson and his Shakespearean Company in *The School for Scandal,* January 4, 1909.

22. Selection of programmes and handbills from the Grand Opera House, Belfast. 1) Handbill for farewell tour of F.R. Benson, 1931. 2) Front detail of Grand Opera House programmes, 1900. 3) Handbill. Carl Rosa Opera Company season. 1917. 4) Programme, The Savoy Players, *The Man Who Came to Dinner,* by George S. Kaufman and Moss Hart, May 3, 1943. 5) Signed photograph of Edward Compton, undated. inscribed 'To R.J. Osborne from a Reformed Rake. 6) Handbill, *Sunny,* December 5, 1927. 7) Souvenir programme of the Grand Opera House, Belfast, 1895–1945. 8) Book of Songs for *Jack in the Beanstalk* December 24, 1931. 9) Programme, Abbey Theatre company on tour with *Juno and the Paycock* by Sean O'Casey. May 21, 1928. 10) Handbill, variety revue, *Brighter Belfast,* May 1929.

23. Bound copies of *The Irish Playgoer* magazine, Dublin 1899.

24. Programme, *The Letter,* by Somerset Maugham, Northern Irish Players at the Empire Theatre, Belfast, 12 June, 1939.

25. Programme, *Workers* by Thomas Carnduff, presented by the Belfast Repertory Company at the Abbey Theatre, Dublin, October 13–15, 1932. Signed by cast and author.

26. Handbill, *Worker.s* by Thomas Carnduff presented by the Belfast Repertory Company at the Empire Theatre, Belfast, November 21, 1932.

27. Selection of programmes from the Hippodrome Theatre. 1) Programme, twice-nightly variety, December 20, 1909. 2) Front detail of programmes during the 1930s. 3) *Cine-Variety No. 5,* featuring variety and film double-bill. 4) Programme, Hippodrome Cinema, January 7, 1935. *Stand Up and Cheer,* featuring Shirley Temple. 5) Programme, Bob Hope at the Royal Hippodrome, 26 May 1951.

Ulster Literary Theatre

Illustrations

28. Covers of *Uladh,* the magazine of the Ulster Literary Theatre, dated February 1905 and September 1905, designed by John Campbell. Centre, signatures of ULT company members and drawing of the foundation meeting of the Ulster Literary Theatre, dated 1904.

29. Photograph of Ulster Literary Theatre production of *The Drone* by Rutherford Mayne, not dated. Set design for same production by H.C. Morrow.

30. Set of photographs of undated Ulster Literary Theatre production of *Thompson in Tír-na-nÓg* by Gerald Macnamara.

31. Drawing by Grace Plunkett of Rutherford Mayne as Cuchulainn in an undated Ulster Literary Theatre production of *Thompson in Tír-na-nÓg* by Gerald MacNamara.

Case Items

32. Programme of the Samhain Festival, 1908, at the Abbey Theatre, Dublin, for which the Ulster Literary Theatre performed *The Flame of the Hearth* by Seamus O'Kelly, and *The Turn of the Road* by Rutherford Mayne.

33. Postcard of the Ulster Literary Theatre to Josephine Campbell inviting her to attend a supper in honour of the Abbey company on December 5, 1908.
34. Original editions of *Uladh,* the magazine of the Ulster Literary Theatre, 1904/5.
35. Signed copy of *The Troth,* by Rutherford Mayne. Dublin: Maunsel and Company, 1909. Inscribed: 'To John P. Campbell, with the compliments of the author. November 11, 1909.'
36. Programme, undated, Ulster Literary Theatre production of *Suzanne and the Sovereigns* by Lewis Purcell and Gerald MacNamara.
37. Programme, Matineee of *The Drone* by Rutherford Mayne, presented by the Ulster Literary Theatre at the Royalty Theatre, London, February 6–16, 1912.
38. First edition of *Thompson in Tír-na-nÓg* by Gerald MacNamara. Dublin: The Talbot Press, [1912].
39. Fragment of poster for Ulster Theatre season at the Playhouse, Liverpool, [1926].

Northern Drama League/Empire Theatre
Illustrations
40. Programme and Certificate for the Northern Dramatic Feis, organised in 1921 by the Northern Drama League at the Empire Theatre Belfast. Certificate signed by Hilton Edwards for presentation to winners, the Carrickfergus Players.
41. Colour poster for the Belfast Repertory Theatre Company premiere of *Machinery* by Thomas Carnduff at the Abbey Theatre, Dublin, March 6, 1933.
42. Two film posters: (top) Paramount British Productions present Richard Hayward in *Irish and Proud of It.* (bottom) Richard Hayward Film Productions Ltd. present Richard Hayward in *Luck of the Irish.* Both 1936.
43. Memorandum of Agreement between Joseph Tomelty and the Empire Theatre of Varieties Ltd. for a stage presentation of *The McCooeys* from December 2, 1956 for two weeks. Dated 21 September 1956.

Ulster Group Theatre
Illustrations
44. Centre: set design an undated Ulster Group Theatre production of George Shiels' *The Old Broom.* Left: poster for Ulster Group Theatre production of *Friends and Relations* by St. John Ervine, May 1944. Right: poster outlining programme from 30 June to 28 July, 1947.
45. Handbill for Northern Ireland Festival Company season at Lyric Theatre, Hammersmith, March 20–April 28, 1951. Below: Undated photograph of one of many Ulster Group Theatre productions of *Boyd's Shop* by St. John Ervine.
46. Caricatures by Rowel Friers of members of the Ulster Group Theatre and the Ulster Theatre Company. Taken from programmes for: 1951 Ulster Group Theatre production of *Arty* by Ruddick Millar and James Mageean, and 1965 Ulster Theatre Company production of *One Year in Marlfield* by Joseph Tomelty.

Case Items
47. Programmes: Ulster Theatre presents *Storm in a Teacup* by James Bridie, March 11, 1940. Harold Goldblatt's Company presents *French Leave* by Reginald Berkeley, March 18, 1940. Northern Irish Players present *Barnum Was Right* by Joseph Tomelty, preceded by *The Bear* by Anton Tchehov, March 25, 1940.
48. Undated photograph of UGT production of *Right Again Barnum* by Joseph Tomelty. John McDaid on left, Jack O'Malley on right.
49. Air Raid Warning notice for audience members, undated.

50. Photograph, BBC Exhibition June 15, 1943. Left to right: J.R. Mageean, Joseph Tomelty, Jack O'Malley, R.H. MacCandless, Mary Braithwait, Eric Holmes, Elizabeth McKeown, Elizabeth Begley, Cicely Mathews, John F. Tyrone, Lynn Doyle (seated).

51. Two letters from George Shiels to David Kennedy, dated 13 May, 1940 and [November 11, 1946].

52. UGT photograph, undated, of the frequently perfommed *Macook's Corner* by George Shiels. Left to right: R.H. MacCandless, Joseph Tomelty, John F. Tyrone, [John McClinton].

53. Signed programme for UGT production of *Boyd's Shop* by St. John Ervine, November 1944.

54. Programme, August 1953 UGT production of *Dust Under Our Feet* by Michael J. Murphy on tour to the London Arts Theatre Club.

55. Programme, UGT Fifth Annual Drama Festival, April 1947.

56. Wages Book for UGT, December 1947 to December 1949, when Joseph Tomelty was General Manager of the theatre.

57. Pencil manuscript of *All Soul's Night* by Joseph Tomelty. Note on cover says 'first draft'.

58. Prompt script kept by Joan Keenan for the 1958 UGT production of *The Bonefire* by Gerard McLamon, directed by Tyrone Guthrie.

59. Handbill for the Ulster Group Theatre C.E.M.A. sponsored Spring Tour 1958 with *Moodie in Manitoba* by George Shiels and *Bachelors Are Bold* by T.M. Watson.

60. Letter from Sean O'Casey to Harold Goldblatt, dated September 29, 1958.

61. Script for first production of *Traitors in Our Way* by Louis MacNeice, March 1957.

62. Postcard, *Wish You Were Here* by John McDonnell, featuring James Young with Jack Hudson, May 1964.

Arts Theatre, Belfast
Illustrations

63. Hand-drawn, laminated poster for *Our Theatre Scrapbook,* an Arts Theatre devised revue staged at the company's Upper North Street venue in June 1950.

64. Photographs, The Arts Theatre, Belfast. Clockwise from top: *The Unknown Woman of Arras* by Armand Salacrou, presented at the Upper North Street premises (undated, pre-1950). Top right: *The Man Outside* by Wolfgang Borchert, presented in 1952 at the Fountain Street venue. Left: Wolsey Gracey and Bryan Hulme in *Waiting for Godot* by Samuel Beckett, the Ulster premiere staged at the Little Donegall Street premises in 1957. Right: *The Country Boy* by John Murphy featuring Mark Mulholland and Bill Hunter, presented by the Ulster Actor's Company at the Botanic Avenue theatre in 1977.

65. Laminated poster for Arts Theatre production of *Huis Clos,* by Jean-Paul Sartre, preceeded by European premiere of *This Property is Condemned* by Tennessee Williams. Staged at Royal Irish Academy Theatre, 36 Westland Row, August 1951.

66. Two Arts Theatre production lists, hand written. *Our Past Productions 1947–1959* and *Our Past Productions 1959–1962.*

Case Items

67. Photograph of Hubert Wilmot, Arts Theatre founder.

68. Programme, Arts Theatre Studio production of *The Unquiet Spirit* by Jean Jacques Bemard at Upper North Street venue. Not dated, but pencilled on front the dates 1947/8.

69. Booklet, *The Stage in Ulster,* featuring article *The Belfast Arts Theatre* by Hubert Wilmot. Belfast: H.R. Carter Publications Ltd., [1951].

70. Programme and photograph for Arts Theatre production of *Point of Departure* by Jean Anouilh at Fountain Street Mews, September 26, 1951.
71. Laminated poster for Belfast Arts Theatre production of *Our Town* by Thornton Wilder at Upper North Street. Not dated, but pre-1950.
72. Laminated poster bill for season August–October 1952 at Fountain Street Mews.
73. Laminated poster for Belfast Arts Theatre production of *The Little Hut* by Andre Roussin and Nancy Mitford at the Little Donegall Street venue, September 1954.
74. Programme, Arts Theatre on tour to City of Derry Drama Club with *Bell, Book and Candle* by John Van Druten in Londonderry Guildhall, February 5/6, 1955.
75. Arts Theatre programme outlines, September–December 1955 and December 1957–January 1958.
76. Handbill for Arts Theatre C.E.M.A. funded touring production of *Anastasia,* adapted from the French of Marcell Maurette by Guy Bolton, January 1955.
77. Promotional photograph for Arts Theatre fundraising campaign for Botanic Avenue theatre. Not dated, late 1950s.
78. Poster for Irish premiere of *Orpheus Descending* by Tennessee Williams. First production in new theatre at Botanic Avenue theatre, April 1961.
79. Programme for Arts Theatre invitation tour to the Abbey Theatre, Dublin, June 19–July 1, 1967 with *The Boys from USA* by Roger Kelly.
80. Programme for Arts Theatre production of *Married Bliss* by Sam Cree, April 19–May 8, 1971.

Lyric Players Theatre
Illustrations
81. Two sketches by George Morrow of 'Beechbank' at 11 Derryvolgie Avenue, Belfast. Published in *The Lyric Players Theatre, 1951–1956.*
82. Caricatures of members of the Lyric Theatre company by Gladys Maccabe, from *The Sunday News,* November 3, 1968.
83. Photograph, *The Street* by John Boyd, produced by the Lyric Theatre, March/April 1977. Cast includes Pat Brannigan, Toby Byrne, Margaret D'Arcy, Catherine Gibson, Des McAleer, Stella McCusker, Joe McPartland, Liam Neeson, Maurice O'Callaghan and Linda Wray. Handbills, *Dark Rosaleen* by Vincent Mahon and *Not I* by Samuel Beckett, produced May 1980; *Dockers* by Martin Lynch, premiered January 1981; *Indian Summer* by Jennifer Johnston, premiered May/June 1983. Photograph, Liam Neeson and Stella McCusker in *The Rise and Fall of Barney Kerrigan* by Frank Dunne, premiered May/June 1977.
84. Costume designs by Anne Whittaker for *The Plough and the Stars* by Sean O'Casey, produced by the Lyric Theatre in November, 1988.

Case Items
85. Drawing by Edward Marley of the Lyric Studio interior. From *The Lyric Players 1951–1959,* published Lyric Players Theatre, 1960.
86. Programmes, Lyric Players Theatre, all 1955/6 season. *Volpone* by Ben Jonson, *The Dark is Light Enough* by Christopher Fry, *The Tragedy of King Lear* by William Shakespeare, and a double-bill, *The Land of Heart's Desire* by W.B. Yeats and Sophocles' *King Oedipus,* a version by W.B. Yeats.
87. Programme for Lyric Players, Belfast Inaugural Dinner at Crawfordsburn Inn, March 1, 1960.
88. Invitation to Alice Berger-Hammershlag for the Lyric Players, Belfast Inaugural Dinner at Crawfordsbum Inn, March 1, 1960.

89. *Threshold,* Volume 1, Number 1, 1967. Publication, *Lyric Theatre 1951–1968,* signed by Austin Clarke. Publication, A *Needle's Eye, The Lyric Players Theatre, Belfast,* 1979.

90. Fundraising brochure, *The Lyric Theatre, Belfast £130,000 Development Programme.* Not dated, late 1960s.

91. Programme for the laying of the Foundation Stone of the new theatre at Ridgeway Street, Belfast, by Austin Clarke, June 12, 1965.

92. Programme, *The Heart's A Wonder,* a musical version of *The Playboy of the Western World* by J.M. Synge, adapted by Mairin and Nuala O'Farrell. At the Grove Theatre, Shore Road, November 1965.

93. Programme, *Four Plays of the Cuchulain Cycle* by W.B. Yeats, dated October 1968.

94. Photograph of Lyric Players Theatre production of *The Playboy of the Western World* by J.M. Synge. dated September/October 1975.

95. Programme for Lyric Theatre production of *The Playboy of the Western World* by J.M. Synge at the Studio, Belfast Waterfront Hall, and at the Lyric Theatre, January 1997.

96. Programme, *Jesus Christ Superstar,* book and lyrics by Timothy Rice, music by Andrew Lloyd Webber. Presented by Lyric Players Theatre, January 1974.

97. Outline of programme for Belfast Academy of Music and Dramatic Art under the auspices of the Lyric Players Theatre Trust, September 1972.

98. Handbill for Lyric Studio production of *The Visit* by Friedrich Durrenmatt, June 1997.

1960s to the present
Illustrations

99. Poster, Field Day Theatre Company. *Double Cross* by Thomas Kilroy, staged by the company at the Lyric Players Theatre, February 12–24, 1986.

100. Poster, Field Day Theatre Company. *Pentecost* by Stewart Parker, staged by the company at the Lyric Players Theatre, October 12–24, 1987.

101. Poster, Charabanc Theatre Company. *Lay Up Your Ends* by Martin Lynch, Marie Jones and the company, at the Group Theatre, Belfast from July 18-30, 1983.

102. Poster, Charabanc Theatre Company. *Somewhere Over the Balcony* by Marie Jones, March 18 and 19, 1988 at the Women in Theatre Festival, Boston College, Robsham Theatre Arts Centre. Photograph (left to right): Marie Jones, Carol Moore, Eleanor Methven.

103. Poster, DubbelJoint Theatre Company. *A Night in November* by Marie Jones, staged at Whiterock Campus, Belfast Institute of Further and Higher Education, August 8–10, 1984 as part of the West Belfast Festival.

104. Poster, *April Sundays,* staged by Tinderbox Theatre Company and Prime Cut (formerly Mad Cow) Productions at the Old Museum Arts Centre, April 1996.

Case Items

105. Script of Sir Tyrone Guthrie for Ulster Theatre Company production of *Macook's Corner* by George Shiels staged in 1969. Programme for same.

106. Programmes. Field Day Theatre Company. World premiere production, *Translations* by Brian Friel, 1980. World premiere, *The Cure at Troy,* by Seamus Heaney after *Philoctetes* by Sophocles, 1990.

107. Invitation, Field Day Theatre Company. *Double Cross* by Thomas Kilroy, February 12, 1986 at the Guildhall, Derry.

108. Two Charabanc Theatre Company Christmas cards, undated.

109. Programme and stage manager's book, Charabanc Theatre Company. *Oul Delf and False Teeth* by Marie Jones and the Company in association with Pam Brighton and Martin Lynch, 1984.
110. Programme, 45th Ulster Drama Festival, May 19–24, 1997 at the Lyric Theatre.
111. Volume XI, *Stage Whispers,* the magazine of the BART players, Christmas 1971.
112. Belvoir Players present *The McCooeys at Christmas, a Hooley In the Kitchen,* by Joseph Tomelty, 1994.
113. Selection of programmes from contemporary companies, including Belfast Theatre Company, Ulster Youth Theatre, Big Telly Theatre Company, Replay Productions, O'Casey Theatre Company, Kabosh, Shanakee, Centre Stage, Point Fields and Ulster Theatre Company.
114. Programme, Ballybeen Community Theatre. *The Mourning Ring,* scripted by Ken Bourke and directed by Paddy McCooey. Performed November 21–25, 1995 at the Dundonald High School, part of the Belfast Festival at Queen's, 1995.
115. Programme, *The Dock Ward Story,* devised by the company. Performed November 16–20, 1991 at St. Kevin's Hall, North Queen Street, Belfast.
116. Programme, DubbelJoint Productions and Just Us Community Theatre. *Bin Lids,* written by Christine Poland, Brenda Murphy, Danny Morrison, Jake MacSiacaiss and other members of the cast, with research by the company. Performed at Belfast Institute of Further and Higher Education, August 5–9, 1997.
117. Shankhill Community Theatre, *Why Susie Smith Didn't Sign On,* writer Rene Greig, not dated.
118. Programme and invitation, Belfast Waterfront Hall. Official Opening Gala Concert, 6 May 1997.